STEP-BY-STEP GARDEN GUIDES

Peter McHoy

Small Gardens

AURA

Step-by-Step Garden Guides Small Gardens

Peter McHoy

© 1997 Aura Books plc
Produced for Aura Books
by Transedition Ltd,
Oxford OX4 4DJ, England

Editing and layout: Asgard
Publishing Services, Leeds

Typesetting: Organ Graphic,
Abingdon

Photographic credits
All photographs by the author.

10 9 8 7 6 5 4 3
Printed in Dubai

ISBN 0 947793 72 0

This small cottage-garden style front garden works harmoniously. Note the unobtrusive low boundary wall.

Peter McHoy has worked on six gardening magazines, three of them as editor, but now devotes most of his time to writing and photography. He has written more than 35 books, most of them on gardening, and contributes regular gardening features to *Park Homes* and *Practical Householder*. He also runs his own horticultural photographic library and acts as consultant to several publishers.

His interest in gardening goes back to childhood — he can remember the excitement of looking over the hedge and being fascinated by a neighbour's greenhouse full of seedlings in spring. This early enthusiasm sparked a particular interest in seeds, and he became a seed analyst before a change of direction took him into publishing over 30 years ago.

His own garden in Sussex is small, so he has encountered most of the problems of gardening in a limited space. But he also knows the benefits of a small garden, especially for anyone with little time to spend in the garden, and that size alone need not limit the pleasures and joy of gardening.

CONTENTS

4 Introduction
Scope and
possibilities 4
Your kind of garden 5
Using this book 7

8 Design sense
Add a dash of
design 8
What's right for
you? 9
Principles of good
design 12
  The exception
  that proves the
  rule 12
  Structural
  principles 12
  Measuring and
  marking 13
  Looking for
  inspiration 14
  Including the
  essentials 15
  Try it out 16
  Open or closed? 17
  Divide to make
  more 18
  Optical illusions 20
  Tips and tricks 21

24 Boundaries
Beautiful and
practical 24
Fences 25
Walls are great 27
Imaginative
solutions 29
Hedges 31

33 The garden floor
Covering the
ground 33
Lawns 34
Non-living ground
cover 36

41 Beds and borders
Showing off the
flowers 41
  Alternatives to
  borders 43
  Make the plants
  work 44

46 Patios and ponds
Patio pleasure 46
Other sitting areas 51
Ways with water 53

56 Containers and ornaments
Containers — a
movable feast 56
Focus on orna-
ments 61
  Focal points 61
  Surprises 62
  Garden art 63
  Throwing light
  on the problem 64

66 The kitchen garden
Growing to eat 66
Vegetables 68
Fruit 71
Herbs 73

75 100 Great small garden plants
Selective shortlist 75
Small broadleaved
trees 76
Small conifers 78
Evergreen shrubs 80
Deciduous shrubs 82
Climbers and wall
shrubs 84
Herbaceous
plants 86
Rock-garden
plants 88
Patio and dwarf
roses 90
Bulbs and corms 92
Container plants 94

96 Index

Scope and possibilities

Your garden may be small in size, but there's no reason why it can't have big impact and be packed with interest. A small garden even has advantages — it will be easier to maintain than a large one, and less expensive to construct and clothe with plants. Your plants will probably receive better attention, and watering, feeding and pest control are all less onerous jobs than they would be in a large garden.

'Small' is a comparative word, of course, a fact that soon becomes obvious if you talk to enough gardeners. What may seem small to someone accustomed to gardening on the grand scale may appear enormous to anyone who normally gardens on a balcony or in a basement garden. In this book are included gardens ranging from the tiny front garden of a town house to a typical back garden found on most modern estates.

In any case, it's not a good idea to get hung up on dimensions, for it is the concepts and ideas that are important. A good idea will probably work as well in a corner of a very large garden as it would in the whole of a small one.

I know all the problems of small-space gardening — my own back garden is only about 30 ft × 30 ft (9 m × 9 m), and the front even smaller. Yet many photographs of parts of it are published in books and magazines every year, so the potential is real. Unfortunately it is constantly being torn apart and remade to try out another idea, so for much of the time it looks more like a builder's yard than an attractive garden!

Few want the effort or the cost of constant redesigning and rebuilding, but with a book like this you can learn from the experiences of others.

The same part of a small garden can be changed to suit different moods and themes, or to bring variety if you get tired of the existing design: **below left** *the gravel phase;* **below** *paving has replaced the gravel.*

Michaelmas daisies and choisya definitely earning their keep in late September

Your kind of garden

This should save you time, money and effort, but above all you may find a speedier route to the garden of your dreams … even if it is a small one.

Make plants work

One of the skills of small-scale gardening is the ability to adapt ideas to suit the scale and size of your own individual garden. Another is to choose appropriate plants.

Plants not only have to be restrained enough for the area they are to occupy, they should also earn their keep by staying interesting most of the time.

Most plants that you use should have a long flowering season, be attractive in leaf for many months, or be 'multi-merit' — perhaps with flowers in spring, berries in autumn, and maybe with the bonus of scent or winter-interest stems.

Single-season borders, such as a spring border or an autumn border, are for the large garden where there is space to develop these ideas and where the focus of interest can move around during the year.

Being selective about the plants should not be restrictive. There are far more suitable ones than you could ever hope to plant if you had dozens of small gardens, let alone just one. The suggested plants starting on page 75 are only a tiny selection of what's available, but you will find them useful as a starting point.

Think first ...

Occasionally a really striking garden simply evolves without any grand scheme. Plants get added, a ornament or a feature is introduced here or there, and somehow the end result is more striking than many planned gardens.

Such gardens are exceptional, however, and usually belong to someone with a natural flair and an 'eye' for what looks right. A garden with a distinctive style — even if it's an abstract one — nearly always looks more pleasing that one that 'just grew'.

Most of us need a thought-out framework, a grand design, or at least a gardening philosophy to work to. A garden added to piecemeal often lacks a sense of coherent design, and a small garden is generally much more difficult to design well than a large one.

You have to think about using space imaginatively but always with caution. All those blank walls and fences can be home for many exciting plants if you think of gardening vertically — but vigorous shrubs may grow inwards as well as upwards, and tall plants around the boundary will cast more shade and may make your small area seem more claustrophobic. It's just a

5

matter of being selective and thinking *before* you plant.

Before becoming consumed with enthusiasm because you like a particular idea or a picture pleases you, pause to decide on the *type* of garden you want to create.

Overriding all your creative design thoughts should be a practical philosophy about the kind of garden you want. Sadly, many gardeners are unclear about this fundamental

point, which is probably why so many gardens seem to fall short of expectations.

Personal preferences

Your garden should reflect *you*. It may not exactly mirror your taste in other things, but it should be the sort of garden you *want* to create ... not what you think others will like. If you want to be eccentric, be so. And don't be deterred by the initial reaction of others.

Is privacy and a sense of enclosure important, or do you find a heavily planted and 'enclosed' garden a trifle claustrophobic? Do you want to screen yourself from neighbours or to be open and create a sense of space beyond?

If you are a plant-lover you will probably want to cram as many plants as possible into your limited space. If minimum maintenance is more important, you probably won't find lots of hard landscaping objectionable, and your choice of plants will be influenced by how much attention (or how little) they need.

Using this book

The aim of this book is to show what can be done where space is limited, and to demonstrate that small gardens needn't lack style or impact. But every garden is different — even where shape and size are similar, the personal preferences of the gardeners are bound to be individual. The best way to use this book is to let it stimulate your thoughts, perhaps to take ideas and adapt them to your own needs, and to try out some of the suggestions and plants.

You will find plenty of advice on simple garden design, but you don't have to redesign your garden to adopt or adapt good ideas. All you need to improve your garden may be the use of a screen, the positioning of an interesting ornament, or the addition of an arbour or overhead beams on a patio to create the illusion of enclosure and privacy.

Use the chapter on boundaries to see whether the perimeter of your garden can be improved. The smaller the garden, the more obtrusive and important a boundary becomes, so getting this right can be crucial to the success of the garden within.

Even in a small garden, the hard landscaping (the paving, walls, and decking, for instance) will form the skeleton that gives the garden

shape, and you will find plenty of imaginative ideas in the garden floor chapter.

When the hard landscaping is to your satisfaction, spend time choosing appropriate plants to enhance it. You will find plenty of ideas here for how to use beds and borders as well as choosing the plants to put in them.

It is often the finishing touches that make a garden special, like the choice and positioning of ornaments or the dramatic effect of garden lighting as darkness falls. You will find many interesting ideas to copy or adapt in the chapter on containers and ornaments.

Don't be afraid to use a few tall plants if they will add a sense of drama as well as beauty. These photographs of fennel illuminated by a spotlight demonstrate how lights used effectively can focus on key features and hide the fact that only a short distance away are the garden fence and other properties.

Add a dash of design

Many small gardens fail to make their mark because they have been dismissed as being too small or too difficult to design.

Yet look at the display gardens at major flower shows, and you will often see 'court-yard', 'town' or 'patio' gardens that are absolutely stunning.

Show gardens and real gardens

'Real' gardens can never be like that, of course — you have to find somewhere to dry the washing, place the refuse bin, and maybe accommodate a garden shed for the clutter that most of us accumulate yet don't want in the house!

Show gardens are often created — at great expense — to look perfect at one point in time. Real gardens are usually a compromise because they have to look reasonable throughout the year. And there is little scope in a small garden for indulging in a series of

seasonal areas screened off from the rest.

Show gardens are always worth studying, however, for they will show you, in a way that words can't, what scope there is for what you may regard as an unpromising plot. Above all, they demonstrate how important design is if you want to transform a small garden into something very special.

Living with your garden's limitations

Every garden — even a large one — has its limitations. It's just that the smaller the garden the more difficult they are to overcome.

- **Boundaries** can't easily be moved, so you have to make a feature of them or disguise them.

- **Lack of privacy** is often a difficult problem to solve, but screening or clever positioning of garden features can work wonders.

- **Shade** is an ever-present problem as there will almost certainly be walls and fences or hedges to cast shadows, but there's a wonderful world of shade plants to be discovered by anyone who takes the trouble.

Once you begin to look at the potential of your garden rather than the negative features, it will suddenly appear much more promising.

Being ruthless

Anyone moving into a new house with an unmade garden has a wonderful opportunity. Most of us have an existing garden, with shrubs or even trees that we may have grown to love, or concreted paths that you will find every excuse not to have to dig up. It takes courage to disregard the existing garden and design it from scratch. It's also much more work — dismantling and moving can take almost as much time as building and planting.

But it *is* worth it — the best and most imaginative gardens come if you explore as many options as possible, in your mind and on paper.

Of course, it makes sense to incorporate as much of the existing garden as possible, but if you *start* with the intention of working the new around the old, an original and creative small garden design will be more difficult to achieve.

The big garden shows usually have display gardens created by some top designers. Don't expect to create gardens to this standard, but take inspiration from them. In this example, designed by David Stevens, there is an important lesson in the use of changing levels.

What's right for you?

Sometimes you can make a garden fence into a feature ... but it depends what lies on the other side.

Many books are written about garden design, and great numbers of enthusiastic amateurs as well as professionals attend garden-design courses in the quest for that elusive quality that sets your garden aside from your neighbours' — even though theirs occupies a similar area.

If you talk to enough enthusiastic gardeners — whether recent converts or life-long devotees — you will realise that beauty is very much in the eye of the beholder, in the garden as elsewhere! One person's pride and joy can be another's turn-off. The only real test is whether your garden is right for you.

In the following pages you will find the basic principles of garden design, but when you see the diversity of great gardens made by designers following similar 'rules', it becomes obvious that it is interpretation that makes the difference. The principles are the 'bones' of good design, but it is how you flesh it out and dress it up that will make your garden unique, with your own individual taste stamped upon it.

Use pictures in books and magazines as inspiration for your own small garden. This one shows how a tiny space can be eye-catching.

9

Personal priorities

It makes sense to spend a little time thinking about the *type* of garden you want before putting pen to paper or spade to soil. It's easy to be carried away with exciting designs that look great — but will they fulfil your expectations long-term? An absolutely stunning garden with a lot of structure but few plants will soon lose its appeal when you're tempted by that wonderful new plant at the garden centre but realise you've nowhere to plant it.

Conversely, there's not much point in creating a cottage garden packed with plants and perhaps a lawn with flower beds if you don't have the time to devote to keeping it looking smart.

Right: *This low-maintenance front garden requires practically no regular care.*

Below: *Lawns look lovely, but they can make your garden high-maintenance.*

Decide whether plants are more important than structure, whether you have time to cut lawns and weed lots of flower beds or whether you would perhaps be better off with a low-maintenance garden with a gravelled area instead of grass, and paving instead of plants.

Bear in mind the setting too. A simple classic design that might look right with an older house to match may look incongruous in a modern semi-detached home on a housing estate. Conversely a modern style of patio garden might sit uneasily alongside a country cottage.

It's a good idea to look at different garden styles, in this book and in magazines, to decide on the *image* you wish to create. You can almost always scale down a theme or style to an appropriate size.

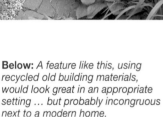

Above: *You don't have to plan a strong design to have a pretty garden. The whole of this small front garden has been given over to what appears to be random planting, with lots of self-sown plants, but it has plenty of impact.*

Below: *A feature like this, using recycled old building materials, would look great in an appropriate setting … but probably incongruous next to a modern home.*

Are you free?

You may not be free to do exactly what you like with your garden, even if you own the property. There may be restrictions placed in the deeds to the property — perhaps drawn up to ensure that open-plan front gardens on an estate remain as the architects and planners intended. In exceptional cases there may be restrictions placed by local authorities or highways departments on the height of hedges, fences and screens — because they might obscure the view for drivers on a bend or corner, for example. The chances are that no such restrictions apply, but it's always worth checking at the planning and dreaming stage!

Principles of good design

The exception that proves the rule

Sometimes chaos (or apparent chaos) works. Some really interesting gardens appear to be a jumble of plants of many kinds grown at random with no apparent structure or design to the paths that meander between them. They usually work because their creators have an 'eye' for plants and an instinctive feel for how to create a natural-looking wilderness of cultivated plants. Such gardens can look fantastic at their best, even if they may be depressing in the off-season. They are for those who feel happiest when things *don't* look designed — but they demonstrate that good gardens don't have to be built to a rigid grid.

Below and **below left:** *The basic rectangular grid to which this tiny garden has been designed can be seen clearly, and it has managed to make the garden really striking.*

Structural principles

The type of garden that most of us would recognise instantly as a 'designed' garden, rather than one that just 'grew' or evolved over time, is likely to have been constructed using traditional design rules.

Large gardens with rolling lawns and large beds and borders can be informal and irregular in design — it is the planting that holds the eye. Small gardens, however, are generally best designed in a more structured way using a grid based on rectangles or circles.

Gardens designed on a grid might sound uninspiring and maybe too formal, but in the finished garden you will probably notice the overall sense of appropriate placement rather than the basic pattern of the grid.

Measuring and marking

Because your garden is small doesn't mean you don't have to measure it. It isn't possible to draw an accurate plan of your garden if you don't have the basic measurements.

Fortunately most small gardens are easy to measure using straight lines, so there's no need to worry about techniques like triangulation to find the position of a tree!

Use the main building or a long straight boundary as the starting point. Then transfer

This patio has been set at a 45° angle to the house, which makes the best use of available sun.

Make your rough sketches and measurements in the garden, so that you have the basic information from which to drawn the outline to scale.

the outline of the building and boundary to a freehand sketch. By measuring from the corners of the building and then taking right angles from these lines, you should be able to pinpoint the corners of beds, the position of major trees that you might want to leave, the garden shed, and mundane but important things like drain inspection covers!

Don't waste time measuring the position of plants or features that you already know you don't want to retain.

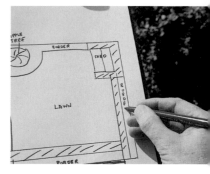

Back indoors, accurately transfer the basic shape of your garden to paper. Graph paper is ideal, and a scale of 1:100, 1:50 or even 1:25 is adequate for most small gardens.

The easiest grid to work with is a rectangular one. Draw lines at appropriate intervals

Computer corner
There are many excellent and relatively cheap garden-design computer programs available. Some will show you what your planned garden will look like at different times of day (complete with shadows) and in different seasons.

These are great fun, but you still need to measure up and come up with the design ideas. However, instead of transferring your measurements to graph paper, key them into your program. Then follow the outline described for the pencil and paper method, but do it on your screen instead.

on your graph paper — say 6 ft (2 m) apart, scaled down of course. If you have a panel fence, it makes sense to make your grid match the position of the fence posts.

You won't want to keep redrawing your master outline, so photocopy it or use tracing paper over the top.

Use the basic grid to lay down the lines of your design. You don't have to make features follow the lines exactly — you can sub-divide the grid to place a bed or a path say half or a third the distance across the basic rectangle. You can even turn the whole design round by 45°, taking your imaginary lines diagonally across the grid.

If you make all your features follow the grid lines (or sub-divisions of them), your garden will have a strong sense of structure. That doesn't mean all the lines have to be at right angles — you can round off corners or mask harsh lines by letting plants blur and soften them.

The grid can also be a series of circles, joined by transitional radii, but this is a more difficult choice to start with, and the scope within a very small garden is limited.

Draw your designs (never be content with the first one!) on the photocopies or overlays until you have something that looks worth pegging out in the garden to help you visualise what it will look like.

Looking for inspiration

Few good small garden designs come as an inspired thought from nowhere. The best are often variations on a theme — adaptations from other designs, made to work in your garden, and modified to reflect your preferences.

Don't spend hours looking at a blank sheet of paper waiting for ideas to appear. Look through the photographs in this book, study pictures in magazines, observe features that you like in gardens in your neighbourhood. Decide what it is you like about the gardens, and see if you can modify the salient features to suit your own garden.

The hard lines of a design based on a rectangular grid can be softened by the appropriate use of plants.

Including the essentials

Drying the clothes

Most of us need somewhere to dry the clothes. In a large garden the clothes drier can be well screened off from the decorative area of the garden. Not so in a small garden,

Left: *This tiny basement-flat garden is full of interest. The use of small-sized paving and gravel ensures that everything looks in proportion. Large-sized paving would have emphasised the garden's smallness.*

Don't worry about the detail at this stage, concentrate on structure and shape — ornaments and individual plants can probably be fitted in later. Try to adapt the elements you like so that they fit within the basic grid structure. Don't be a slave to the grid, however. If you want a cottage-garden style, it will have little formal structure, and the important thing will be the choice of plants and how you position them.

If you can fit existing paths and structures into your plan, that's a bonus. If you aren't prepared for some hard work moving apparent 'fixtures', forget about a fundamental redesign and concentrate on making the best of what you have with the imaginative use of plants and ornaments.

If you don't want to alter the structure of your existing garden, it might be possible to give it more character by the tasteful use of ornaments.

where a large rotary drier can dominate everything. If you take into account the space required around the drier to allow for sheets to flap in the wind, the handicap is even greater.

The only practical place for a rotary drier is in a paved area, and provided you are prepared to remove it from its socket after use each time, it needn't spoil your garden.

A clothes line may be more appropriate, especially if you are prepared to take the line

Think about the practical things — like somewhere to put the refuse — when designing your garden.

down after use. Unfortunately the washing line traditionally runs down the centre of the garden, perhaps along the line of a path. This is sure to cut your garden in half visually and make it look very 'ordinary'. Move the line to one side, or perhaps across the garden, even if it makes it shorter.

Plan the clothes drier or line into your design, but don't design your garden around it!

Garden shed

The garden shed is even more of a problem, unless you can tuck it out of sight down the side of the house or in some other inconspicuous place where it won't impinge on your design.

If you simply have to live with it, see if you can move the shed rather than having to design around it. It might be possible to screen it with a trellis, cover it with climbers, or even make it into a decorative feature by painting it a cheerful colour and giving it windowboxes.

Think laterally if you can't move an unattractive feature such as a shed or a utility area. Try taking the eye away from it by creating a focal point in front of it or to one side. If you place a pond or running water, or use containers with very bright flowers, in front of the problem structure, you may be surprised at how effectively the eye is taken by the focal point and how the less attractive background is subconsciously ignored.

Try it out

Before spending money and considerable effort redesigning your garden, try pegging out the modifications with canes and string — or maybe a hosepipe if you want curves. This will soon show up short-comings like paths that looked ample on paper but that look mean and narrow in reality.

Leave your marked-out garden for a few days — certainly until you have been able to observe the shadows on a bright day. You may change your mind about the position of the patio, or decide that the plants in a particular border will have to be shade-lovers.

A lawn does not have to be large to have impact. It's the quality of the turf that makes it eye-catching.

Only when you are convinced that your garden improvements will be just that should you spend money and begin physical reconstruction.

Open or closed?

Many small gardens on housing estates are open-plan — they have no enclosing boundary hedges or fences. Planners and designers sometimes stipulate that this must be maintained to give the area a sense of unity and to prevent homeowners creating gardens that do not fit in with the other homes in the neighbourhood.

Even if you are not allowed to have fences or boundary hedges, there remains enormous scope for creative gardening. Make the most of beds and borders — you can even create an effective screen by planting shrubs towards one side, and if you can persuade your neighbour to do likewise you will have a similar

 Shade is a particular problem for small gardens. In a large garden there are almost sure to be sunny areas, but most parts of a small garden are in the shade of the dwelling or fences, not to mention trees, for at least part of the day.

effect to a hedge but with something visually much more interesting.

To give the impression of a heavily planted area, use plenty of climbers and wall shrubs against the wall, use attractive shrubs in large tubs by the door or drive, and plant flower beds with lots of low-growing shrubs. Leave space for seasonal plants too, to add variety and colour, but avoid using *only* seasonal plants otherwise the garden will look flat and bleak for many months of the year.

Making low rock outcrops will provide an opportunity to grow a large range of rock plants without spoiling the scale or sense of openness. Ponds also provide high impact without spoiling a low-level profile.

The quality of a lawn is more important than its size. A small but really high-class lawn, complete with those classic

stripes, will have more impact than a mediocre one many times its size in a large garden.

Fortunately most of us have the opportunity to enclose our gardens if we so wish, yet paradoxically the best way to improve an enclosed garden may be to get rid of the old hedge or close-board fence!

Fences usually make a small area seem even smaller, and hedges are even more of a problem. It is not uncommon for a hedge to be 18 in (45 cm) across, and even allowing for half that width being in your neighbour's garden, you could be losing valuable planting space in a small garden. Hedges also impoverish the soil around the base, making it difficult to grow plants close up to them.

You could achieve a similar effect by making a 'fedge' — erecting a wire mesh fence and covering it with an evergreen climber such as ivy. This gives

If your neighbour has an attractive garden too, you may want to consider a minimum-obstruction fence like this. It will give the impression that your own garden is larger than it is.

Divide to make more

It may not seem logical to divide a small garden into even smaller areas, but it's a practical way to give your garden a sense of mystery and imagination. A garden that's little more than a flat area surrounded by a boundary is in danger of looking boring because the whole garden can be taken in at a glance. Dividing it up into separate visual areas or zones

you the screen without the width. Simply clip the ivy back with shears if it becomes too bushy.

If your neighbour has an attractive garden, however, there's a lot to be said for eliminating solid boundaries and erecting a few token posts and a rail or chain boundary marker. You can still provide visible and psychological boundaries with borders along the perimeter, and the plants will benefit by receiving more light and moisture than they would get near a hedge or fence.

Alternatively, think about making a feature of your boundary. Brick walls can be very attractive if interesting bonds are used; stone walls even more so. Fences can also

be attractive in their own right, and some of these are described on pages 25-26.

Below: *This trellis, covered with honeysuckle, divides this small back garden into two parts, so that you have to explore a little to see it all.*

18

is one of the most effective ways to make a small garden more interesting. And the technique works whether you place the emphasis on hard or soft landscaping.

Creating garden 'rooms' is a popular concept, but making them with tall hedges or even trellis screens may make your garden seem claustrophobic if it's really small, and will take up valuable planting space. You can achieve a similar effect by making low raised beds and using changes of level.

It's the fact that you have to walk around the garden (and can discover different facets of the garden in the process) that makes the difference. Try to make a garden that has to be explored, or at least one where you have to view the garden from different angles to appreciate all its secrets.

It's a good idea to have at least part of the garden that can't be viewed without the effort of exploration. It may be possible to use a trellis clothed with climbers to provide height without the barrier being too

Using a trellis with 'windows' to divide up an area ensures a sense of exploration without blocking out too much light.

oppressive. Keep the plants trimmed, however, otherwise the effect will be lost and the area screened can become gloomy with a lot of shadow in a small space. Try using a trellis with cut-out areas through which you can view the garden beyond — this can make a dividing trellis more acceptable, as can using a trellis with a shaped top rather than a straight top rail.

The tinier the garden, the more difficult it is to use any kind of screen to divide up your garden, in which case it may be best to abandon this kind of visual device. Instead,

concentrate on breaking up the area with different textures. A formal pond that divides an area with water as a texture imparts impact without height. Blocks of ground cover plants can have a similar effect.

Optical illusions

Much can be done with optical illusions to make a limited space seem larger.

Mirrors

Many tricks can be done with mirrors … in the garden as elsewhere. In a walled garden, try putting a mirror in a false doorway set into the wall, or even use a mirror on the back of a real solid gate. It must, of course, fill the whole of an arched frame, otherwise the illusion is broken.

To work well, the mirror also needs to reflect an attractive part of the garden — you don't want to double unattractive features such as the garden shed!

A mirror at the end of a pond that has been taken up to a

Using a mixture of different paving materials will add a lot of interest to your garden. But be careful not to overdo it!

wall can also look deceptively real with the water apparently continuing beyond.

Try introducing a small bridge at the back of a pond taken up close against a boundary. If you place a mirror beneath the bridge it will look as though the water flows out of the garden.

There are problems with mirrors. You must keep them clean, and some gardeners are concerned about their effect on birds, which sometimes fly into them. (At least this shows that the illusion works!)

Perspective
Try making your garden path taper towards the end of the garden — it will make it seem longer. You can't easily do this with bricks or paving slabs, but it's feasible with gravel or grass. If you put a focal point, such as an ornament, close to the ground, this may also help with the illusion.

Masking the boundaries
Try to hide the boundaries in some way by using shrubs or other plants to mask them. If fences or boundary hedges are what the eye sees from both main and peripheral vision, it will emphasise the smallness of your garden. By planting shrubs along the sides and the end, but with the corners filled in with denser planting brought into the garden, the eye will be less conscious of the boundaries. By bringing some shrubs further into the garden part-way along the edge, it may be possible to suggest that the garden extends beyond the true boundary on that side.

Bricks and pavers are excellent construction materials for a small garden.

Tips and tricks
Make the most of different surfaces. An area of timber decking adjoining a paved area, and perhaps with a smart green lawn — or gravel instead if you prefer — can give the impression of many elements without in any way making the garden appear smaller.

Avoid the use of large paving slabs in a small garden. The smaller the unit of paving the larger the paved area will seem. Bricks are ideal for the hard landscaping of small gardens.

Unless you particularly want a low-maintenance garden with few plants (you can have low maintenance *and* plenty of plants if you choose them carefully), don't skimp on the vegetation. Just choose plants

in proportion to the size of your garden. And be sure to use a good sprinkling of evergreens so that fences are not exposed excessively when the leaves fall.

Trees
Don't avoid trees totally. They give a garden a sense of maturity and a crucial vertical dimension. Just select them carefully, going for naturally small trees and if possible multi-merit ones too. Many ornamental crab apples have flowers, fruit, and good autumn tints, for example, and an amelanchier grown as a tree has masses of flowers, sometimes berries, and almost always has autumn colour.

Use slow-growing fastigiate (narrow, columnar) trees. The

golden yew *Taxus baccata* 'Fastigiata Aurea' is one example, but for a faster-growing plant try the flagpole cherry (*Prunus* 'Amanogawa').

Even in tiny gardens there is usually space for a slow-growing weeping tree like the Kilmarnock willow (*Salix caprea pendula*, now more correctly named *S.* 'Kilmarnock') or a Camperdown elm (*Ulmus glabra* 'Camperdownii') or even a weeping purple beech (*Fagus sylvatica* 'Purpurea Pendula')!

By using a visually strong feature like this bubble fountain (**opposite**), *it may be possible to draw the eye away from the limitations of a garden's small size and close boundaries.*

Good and bad views

If you have a good view beyond the garden, or if your neighbour has an attractive garden in a style that matches your own, consider a minimum-obstruction fence (see page 24) so that the eye is taken beyond your own domain.

If, however, the view beyond is something you want to hide, use screens, but also use devices to draw the eye *within* the garden. This can be achieved by making the main focal point close to the centre of the garden — perhaps a sundial or a circular patio with super sunshade, or a water feature such as a bubble fountain.

Use plenty of subsidiary focal points around the garden, with the emphasis on those that take the eye downwards.

A flowering crab apple (Malus floribunda) sets off this small front garden nicely.

Feature checklist

It makes sense to compile a checklist of features that are important to you, to take into account at the design stage. Inevitably some of them will have to be dropped, but try to incorporate as many as possible of those you have rated as essential or important.

Feature	Essential	Important	Desirable	Not wanted
Barbecue (built-in)				
Clothes drier				
Dustbin hide				
Garden seat(s)				
Gravel area				
Greenhouse				
Herb garden				
Lawn				
Patio/sitting area				
Rock garden				
Summerhouse				
Tool shed				
Water feature				

Beautiful and practical

Boundaries are a problem whatever the size of your garden. If it's large they are expensive to build and maintain — not to mention time-consuming if there are long hedges to cut; if it's small the boundary will almost always impinge on your consciousness. They also cause practical problems, such as shade, and dryness in the 'rain shadow'.

There are, after all, advantages to 'open plan' gardens where traditional hedges and fences are abolished.

Invisible boundaries

If you are fortunate enough to live in the countryside with fields or an attractive view beyond, let your garden act as a window. Thin and inconspicuous wires or low chain-link can serve as a boundary marker without spoiling the view. It might even be possible to dispense with any above-ground obstruction by using a ditch to mark the edge of your garden. This can act like a small-scale version of the ha-ha that you can still see on large estates.

Visible but unobtrusive

Most of us want privacy, of course, so in many situations we need something more than a mere boundary-marker. In a town, where gardens are normally overlooked by neighbours, this can be particularly

important. The skill lies in choosing a boundary that provides privacy and serves its practical functions (keeping dogs and children out perhaps) without being visually obtrusive.

This low chain-link is all that is needed to mark the boundary.

Where a proper functional boundary is needed, there are two principal ways to approach the problem:

- use camouflage — clothe the boundary with climbers or hide it with evergreen shrubs, for example

- or make a feature of it, which demands more imagination but can make your garden look that little bit special.

Fences

Small but smart

Picket fences are the easiest type of boundary to construct if you want one that looks good without giving the garden a sense of being too enclosed. You can make your own or buy them as kits. Although traditionally made of wood, you can also obtain plastic versions.

This type of fence, with its spaced 'pales' nailed to horizontal bars, have connotations of old country cottage gardens, yet they can look good on a modern housing estate too. They are usually 3–4 ft (90–120 cm) high, so they never look out of proportion in a small space.

If you leave the wood plain, the fence will recede visually, which may be what you want. On the other hand, if you want to make a feature of it, a picket fence can be very decorative if

painted. The traditional colour is white, but of course in this case you must repaint it periodically and wash it down a couple of times a year, otherwise the impact is lost. You could be even more adventurous and paint or stain the wood green or blue.

Picket fences usually have pointed spear-like pales at the top, but they can be shaped in a variety of ways, perhaps rounded or formed into finials. Attention to details like this

Picket fences are usually painted white, but don't have to be. This one has been painted green, and is unusual because it's a hybrid between a picket and a hit-and-miss fence, which makes it a little more animal-proof. (A hit-and-miss fence is one where slightly overlapping vertical boards are fixed on alternate sides of the supporting timber.)

will improve the fence as a feature.

A picket fence by itself will not provide much privacy, but shrubs planted in front or behind it will prevent it being 'see through'.

Ranch fencing — broad white horizontal planks fixed to stout upright posts — is another good choice for a small garden, especially if backed by low-growing shrubs to about

Ranch fencing can look smart and you can still see plenty of plants through it. This one is a plastic version.

the height of the fence or a little taller. Again these fences are not normally more than 4 ft (1.2 m) tall, and the generous space between the planks means you can see plenty of plants though the fence.

Wood is the traditional material for ranch fencing; it should be painted white to look smart. You can also get modern plastic versions that look very convincing and need less maintenance. Instead of painting them, you just go over them with soap and water when they're looking grubby.

Consider building a bamboo fence if you're creating a garden in the Japanese style, or just because it appeals to you.

Something unusual

Fences may seem boring at first sight, but they are a fascinating subject once you begin to study them. If you keep your eyes open, especially when travelling abroad, the possibilities will be quite exciting. Just of few of the more unusual kinds suitable for a small garden are described and illustrated here, but be prepared to experiment if you see something elsewhere that you like.

If you have a modern or abstract style of garden, you could use wooden **railway sleepers** set on end. This may sound horrendous, but in the right setting they can give a garden a striking individual look. Make sure they are sawn off to different heights to provide variety, and of course they must be securely anchored for stability. Old

railway sleepers are available from a number of suppliers.

If you have a Japanese-style garden, why not build a **bamboo fence**? Obtaining the materials and constructing a bamboo fence can be a bit daunting, but books on Japanese gardening are available to help.

A rustic or sawn timber **trellis** could look attractive in a rural setting, especially if the garden beyond is attractive enough.

Above: *Why not use your fences productively? These are cordon pears, but cordon apples are also very successful against a fence.*

Walls are great

Few gardeners bother to build walls, but you may already have one if you live in an old property or a newer one where the builders have not taken the cheaper and easier option of fences.

Tall walls are a challenge most likely to be faced in

basement gardens or old town properties with walled back yards. These *can* be daunting to deal with, but improving them isn't difficult.

Try painting them white or cream, for a start, using masonry paint. This will reflect more

light, which not only benefits the plants but will also make your small enclosed area seem less gloomy.

Use plenty of wall shrubs and climbers, but if you have painted the wall it's best to fix hinged trellises against which the climbers can grow. When the wall needs a fresh coat of paint, try lowering the trellis for access. Some plants will be flexible enough to allow this, others will not.

If you already have well-established climbers and wall shrubs that make it difficult to

If you inherit a large, drab wall, try a coat of masonry paint — it can work wonders.

paint the brickwork, try painting just part of the wall. If you want to be really bold, try a series of white circles, perhaps increasing or decreasing in size as you work up the wall. It will certainly make your walled garden look distinctive and far from mundane.

Garden walls about 4-6 ft (1.2-1.8 m) tall make a great backdrop for trained fruit trees such as cordon or espalier

If you are faced with an unattractive view like this (left), try to screen it ...

A feeling of privacy can also be created by small trees and tall shrubs around the boundary. For some this would be claustrophobic and take up space required for more colourful flowers. But others of us like the sense of seclusion and intimacy that this 'leafy' type of garden creates. And a garden that is so thickly planted with permanent plants that you can't even see the boundary will also filter out noise and bring its own sense of calmness, even in a city setting.

This kind of garden requires skill with the choice of shade-loving plants, the use of plenty of ornaments and focal points within the garden, and dramatic features like garden lights.

Simply by placing a tree in a large pot you can begin to block out the unattractive features.

This is a specimen of a Norway maple, Acer platanoides *'Drummondii', only one year after planting, and it will gradually block out more ... yet because it's in a container the tree will not become too large.*

The ugly bare fence to the left is now masked in summer by a golden hop (Humulus lupulus 'Aureus').

A **screen-block wall** at one end of your sitting area, perhaps clothed with shrubs to soften the harshness, will also offer a little extra seclusion without the oppressiveness of a solid wall. Screen blocks, also known as pierced blocks, are those building blocks that have been pierced with shaped holes to form a decorative pattern.

In a very tiny garden a patio overhead may not be appropriate, but you can usually find space for an **arbour**. This feature will make an excellent focal point while providing a small area of seclusion where you can sit to enjoy your garden.

Hedges

The problem with hedges is that they take up space (they are much thicker than a fence), and the traditional evergreens can look gloomy and oppressive in a small garden. Hedges can look smart and be attractive, however, and it is just a question of choosing an appropriate one.

Feature hedges

Golden hedges are usually more attractive than green ones. The shrubby honeysuckle *Lonicera nitida* makes a far more interesting hedge in its golden form 'Baggesen's Gold' than the plain green species. A golden privet will likewise look lighter and brighter than the green form.

Above: *An informal flowering hedge, like a floribunda rose, may be more appropriate for a small garden than a traditional evergreen hedge.*

Informal hedges are often less 'enclosing' than formal ones, and therefore more acceptable in a small front garden. Look at alternatives to traditional boundary hedges — you can use almost anything that appeals.

Some shrub roses, such as *Rosa rugosa,* are easily kept compact and have beautiful summer flowers followed by large red hips in the autumn. Shrubby potentillas will flower for most of the summer, and many deciduous berberis have the bonus of flowers in spring and small berries in the

Even common hedging plants look more interesting if you choose a golden form, and they are usually a little slower-growing. This one is Ligustrum vulgare 'Aureum' (the golden privet).

31

autumn. Some, like *B. thun-bergii* 'Atropurpurea', have colourful foliage, while many of them have attractive autumn colouring before the leaves fall.

A hedge that borders a pavement does not have to be tall to serve its function. A low-growing lavender hedge can look very smart, won't cast much shade, and certainly won't make your garden look too enclosed.

Sometimes a formal, neatly trimmed, hedge is right, but it doesn't have to be high. There are dwarf forms of some traditional hedge-plants, such

as the edging box *Buxus sempervirens* 'Suffruticosa', and compact versions of berberis, such as *B. thunbergii* 'Atropurpurea Nana'. These are ideal where scaled-down hedges are required.

Full-sized traditional hedges like privet and yew can be more acceptable for a small garden if you shape the top into a wedge. This makes it look more 'special', and also helps to cast a little less shade for a given height.

Hedges are often wider than they need to be. Even old hedges can often be rejuvenat-

ed by cutting them back almost to the centre, and then keeping the new growth trimmed back. Don't try this with conifers other than yew, however, and only cut back one side of any hedge in a year — tackle the other side once the first side has made some new growth.

Compact varieties of berberis make good small hedges. This is a specimen of Berberis thunbergii *'Bagatelle'.*

Covering the ground

What carpets the ground between the flower beds is something that flower-lovers probably think of last — yet the garden floor probably has more impact on your garden than the flower beds! It's what you have to look at all year round, long after the transient flowers are over.

The lawn, and alternatives to grass, can be what sets the flowers off. A great lawn can make even a mediocre garden look good, and can place a good garden among the best. But don't feel compelled to have grass if the size of your garden makes it inappropriate.

Making the right choice

The type and amount of ground cover affects how much time you have to spend on maintenance. You can use ground-cover plants to cut down on weeding, yet a lawn will demand more time and effort to keep in good shape than it takes to keep a flower bed weeded.

What is right for one garden may be wrong for another, but at least time spent thinking about how you are going to carpet the garden floor will reduce the risk of making wrong choices.

A circular lawn is likely to be more of a feature than a rectangular one, but of course it will be more troublesome to mow.

Lawns

The smaller the lawn, the more difficult it can be to maintain in good condition. Unless the design means it is purely decorative, with paths around it and perhaps stepping-stones across it, a small lawn will have to take concentrated wear and tear.

A striped effect may be difficult to achieve if there is too much 'turning area' needed for the mower in relation to the long, straight run, but you can cheat by combing the grass to or from the edge with a stiff brush to extend the stripe right up to the edge.

Shade from hedges and buildings can encourage moss and may also cause dry patches where growth is poor.

Rectangular lawns in small gardens have to be top quality if they are to enhance the garden and not detract from its beauty. Bear in mind that in summer there may be water restrictions that mean you can't use a hose, so that lovely green sward may become a brown patch at the heart of your garden. No matter how bright the flowers, it will detract from them.

If you can be sure of keeping your grass lush and green, try making more of a feature of it by making it a distinctive shape. It could be L-shaped or round, for example, or even run diagonally across the garden.

Not all lawns are intended to be decorative, and if you just need a play area for the children and somewhere to park your garden furniture on a nice day, use a hard-wearing grass mixture and place the emphasis beyond the lawn, with flower beds or other focal points to hold the interest.

A chamomile lawn is the most popular alternative to grass, but it's best confined to a small area.

Alternatives to grass

Grass is so widely used because it's the best choice when it comes to year-round performance and tolerance to wear. It also has less obvious advantages over the other living alternatives — like being able to control weeds with a selective weedkiller rather than having to do back-breaking hand weeding!

However, if you have difficulty growing good grass, consider one of the alternatives, ideally grown in a small decorative area that won't take much wear.

The first plant that most gardeners turn to as an alternative to grass is **chamomile** (*Chamaemelum nobile*, still widely sold under its older

34

Living carpets
Very tiny gardens, where a grass lawn is impractical, can simply be carpeted over with a single type of ground-cover plant. *Pachysandra terminalis* is a good choice as it will produce a dense mat of growth to an even height. Such living carpets create a richer texture than paving, and aren't that much more work once they are well established.

Try planting a small tree or something with a little height to prevent the area looking too boring — *Cotoneaster* 'Hybrida Pendula' grown as a weeping standard is compact enough for even a *really* tiny garden.

name of *Anthemis nobilis*), popular because it is fragrant when crushed. The variety usually grown is 'Treneague', because it does not normally flower. A flowering chamomile lawn is like a grass lawn full of white daisies — something you find either pretty or abhorrent, depending on your point of view.

Chamomile has the advantage of being widely available, but sending off for small plantlets by mail order may be a much less expensive option than buying plants in pots from garden centres.

Thyme is another popular choice. Choose the creeping thyme (*Thymus serpyllum*).

There are less obvious choices, like some of the fairly rampant **cotulas**, such as *C. potentilliana* and *C. squalida*. These are sometimes regarded as weeds in fine turf, but on their own it doesn't matter.

Don't dismiss plants that we normally consider as lawn weeds, provided you can contain them in a small area! Moss is something that most of us try to eliminate, but if you have a Japanese-style garden, a moss 'lawn' can look superb.

Clover in a lawn is usually treated with weedkiller, but if you leave it you will notice how green it remains after the grass has turned brown in very dry weather. You could try a

small clover lawn — it may remain greener than the grass lawns of your neighbours during the driest months of summer. You may have to go to a specialist seedsman or agricultural seed specialist to obtain the seed. Wild white clover is the type to try.

If your garden is very small, it may be best to plant ground cover like this Pachysandra terminalis, *rather than bothering with a lawn.*

Non-living ground cover

Go for gravel

You don't have to pave your garden if you decide to do without a lawn. Gravel can look superb in the garden, and there are so many kinds, in different sizes, shapes and colours (which also vary with the light and depending on whether it is wet or dry), that you should have no difficulty in finding one that blends in with the rest of the garden.

Gravel has the great advantage of being low-maintenance. There's no cutting to be done as there is with a lawn, and weeds are seldom a problem, provided that the ground is cleared of perennial weeds first and that you lay the gravel at least 2 in (5 cm) thick. If you lay the gravel on a sheet of thick polythene, this will minimise the risk. You can still plant through the polythene if

necessary. If a few seedlings do germinate they can usually be destroyed by raking the gravel, otherwise a path weedkiller applied once a year is usually sufficient to wipe them out.

The more you use gravel, the more you will begin to appreciate its merits. The different varieties all have their charm.

This gravelled area is a straight replacement for the grass that was there before. There's no mowing now!

Left *and* **below left:** *You can plant very effectively through gravel.*

of wired split-log edging, to keep the gravel in place.

Gravel can also make a useful infill between areas of paving, helping to create changes of texture.

Planting through gravel

With small-space gardening it's necessary to make use of every planting opportunity. By filling in spaces between paving slabs with gravel, you can plant areas that would otherwise lack the softening effect of plants. Alongside paths it's best to use 'carpeters' (i.e. low-growing plants that spread to form a carpet) that tolerate being trodden on and yet are not too rampant, such as thymes and *Sagina subulata* 'Aurea', but in less vulnerable areas there are many more possibilities, such as the various rock phloxes and dianthus.

A larger gravelled area, perhaps replacing a conventional lawn, can look a bit bleak without plants to soften the effect. Low-growing plants can be planted through the gravel around the edge, and it's a good idea to plant a whole group of plants, rather like a bed, in places where the garden appears to lack colour or interest.

Simply pull back the gravel, making slits through the polythene if used, and plant

It has many practical advantages too. It will fit any space, no matter how awkward, without the need for cutting like bricks or slabs … and unlike paving you can plant through it! These are major benefits in a small garden, where space is tight and full use has to be made of every available corner.

You can use gravel as a straight replacement for grass, retaining the normal lawn shape with a small raised edge to prevent the gravel from scattering. Use concrete coping or path edging, or even lengths

37

If a garden is very tiny, gravel can look really good. The plants in this photograph are still quite young, however, and will have to be pruned back eventually to prevent them covering the gravel completely.

Dispel decking doubts

Timber decking — planks of wood nailed or screwed to a supporting framework — is another alternative ground-cover medium to consider. It is not a popular choice in the UK, but the merits of decking are widely appreciated in Scandinavia and the USA, for example.

Decking is sometimes very elaborate, and may even be raised above the surrounding ground on pillars where it slopes. In a small garden its use is usually more modest, replacing the more common paving slabs for a patio, or maybe bringing interest to an otherwise featureless corner.

You can be adventurous and stain it various colours, or

normally. If topsoil has been removed and only subsoil remains, be sure to enrich the planting areas with moisture-retaining material such as garden compost and plenty of slow-acting fertiliser. Replace the gravel after planting.

Tall and striking plants like verbascums and angelica can be grown in gravelled beds, but in a small garden it's best to restrict most of the planting to low-growing perennials such as helianthemums, *Oenothera missouriensis*, thrift (*Armeria maritima*) and dianthus. The last two are particularly useful because they are evergreen and it's important to have some plants that look good in the winter months.

Make the most of the areas by planting autumn-flowering bulbs like colchicums and *Crocus speciosus*, and spring miniatures such as *Narcissus bulbocodium* or *Tulipa tarda*. Dwarf bulbs can look very natural growing in this kind of setting, and they will help to extend the period of interest.

leave it a more natural weathered wood colour — it depends on the setting. The one essential is to use good-quality timber that has been pressure-impregnated with a preservative (talk to your timber merchant and explain what you want the wood for). And of course the framework must keep the timber out of direct contact with the ground. If you follow those basic rules, decking could bring a touch of class to your garden, no matter how small it is.

Timber is a very 'sympathetic' material for garden use, and decking makes a pleasant change from paving slabs or pavers.

If you have doubts about the timber or how to make a deck, try one of the companies specialising in this kind of 'garden floor'.

Small paving units look better than large ones in a small garden. Here pavers have been used and combined with gravel for a really pleasing effect.

Paving can be pleasing

Paths and areas of paving are what give your garden structure, and they are almost certain to play a more important role in a small garden than in a large one.

Large, plain paving slabs are not the ideal choice for a small garden. They somehow manage to look drab and boring while at the same time being surprisingly conspicuous. Choose textured finishes, and try mixing different materials (such as paving slabs interspersed with bricks) or just using small-sized paving units such as bricks or pavers.

Generally, the smaller the size the paving material, the more in proportion it will seem in a small garden.

Try to use the same or a similar paving unit for the paths as for the patio, to give the garden an integrated look. If possible, introduce a few small changes of level, but try to use the same material for the steps. Changes of texture are important, but too many changes of paving material in a very small area can be disconcerting. If you decide on a combination of materials, try to use the same combination through a large part of the garden.

Inspection covers

The best-laid plans can be spoilt by something as mundane as a drain inspection cover. Somehow show gardens never seem to have drain covers to contend with! You may even have several of them if you are unfortunate. While they may go almost unnoticed in a large garden, you will be aware of them constantly in a small one. Don't try to hide a drain inspection cover by standing a container on top — it will not hide it completely and will only draw attention to it.

If the cover occurs in a border it's relatively simple to screen it with shrubs — but remember that you must leave access, so don't plant a prostrate shrub to cover it. The big problem arises in lawns and areas of paving. You can use a drain cover with a planting trough, but laying grass in that will only be partially effective unless you can be sure the soil won't dry out. It's better to design your garden so that the covers don't mar your lawn.

Inspection covers in paved areas are much easier to deal with. Buy a special inspection cover designed with a shallow trough in which you can lay the bricks or paving. If you cut them neatly with an angle grinder or block splitter, the effect should be pleasing. You will still be able to see the outline of the tray, but the eye will tend to pass over the area instead of being drawn towards it.

Drain inspection covers are always a problem, but you can buy special covers that are like a tray to hold your pavers or paving slabs. This is more acceptable than a metal cover within a paved area.

Showing off the flowers

Flower beds and borders are what most of us think about when gardens are mentioned. No matter how clever the design, or how impressive the hard landscaping, raised beds, pergolas and other structures,

it's the plants that make a garden.

Unfortunately the traditional long flower borders demand space and time, and are to be admired in grand gardens rather than attempted in small

back yards. And the fussy flower beds cut into the front lawn and packed with summer-flowering and later spring-flowering bedding plants have gone out of fashion — though if they appeal there is no reason why you should not recreate the heydays of traditional bedding.

Difficult choices have to be made, however. There's so much choice nowadays, with a huge range of herbaceous plants and shrubs, and tender overwintered 'patio plants' sold for summer garden decoration, as well as a bewildering array of seed-raised bedding plants and bulbs. In a small garden there's a limit to how many plants you can pack in.

For that reason, dedicated shrub borders and herbaceous borders are increasingly rare. Mixed borders are the order of the day, with shrubs and herbaceous plants grown together, bulbs, corms and tubers packed into any gaps between them, and annuals used to fill in the few remaining spaces. Such mixed borders not only look attractive for a long period, they also avoid bare or uninteresting areas during the winter months when a traditional herbaceous border would look uninspiring at best.

In a small garden, mixed borders containing both shrubs and herbaceous plants, and even annuals, are more practical than separate borders for each kind of plant.

41

Try naturalising suitable small bulbs like these anemones in the lawn at the edge of the border. It's another example of making the most of available space, and will make your border seem bigger when the bulbs are in flower. ('Naturalising' bulbs means planting them where they can grow and multiply undisturbed.)

narrow beds around each edge with a rectangular lawn in the middle: you can be more imaginative than that.

Simply bringing the corners out into the lawn in broad sweeps can make the garden look more designed and provide extra planting area at the same time. If you plant bulbs in the grass and leave them to grow naturally in drifts

This 'cottage garden' was created at the Chelsea Flower Show in 1988, but it captures the essentials of this type of traditional garden. There is no complicated structural design, just broad beds and a straight path. All the creativity goes into the choice and juxtaposition of the plants.

Island beds

Island beds (as opposed to one-sided borders) also have their drawbacks exposed in a small garden. They work well where there is space, but taking an island bed out of a small or narrow garden could emphasise the limitations. You may be glad to have borders running along a boundary to help hide the fence or give the illusion of greater depth, but avoid ribbon beds. Bring them out into the lawn in sweeps and bays, or in steps if the area is paved.

In a small, square garden, you could create a circular lawn or patio in the centre with flower beds all around on three sides, giving great depth at the corners for taller or bigger plants.

Front gardens

Front gardens are more difficult to design with beds and borders in mind. Practical things — boundaries, paths, and perhaps a drive for the car — all impinge and constrain. But try to avoid the standard

near to the borders (not lifting them each season), this will also give the impression of more planting space.

Don't assume that complicated designs or shapes for beds and borders are necessarily the best. It depends on the style of garden you want to create. If you want to make a cottage garden, two straight and wide borders, one either side of a central path, may be all that's necessary, together with a picket fence, perhaps, an attractive gate and a rose or honeysuckle arch around the door. It is the choice of plants and how they are planted that makes this kind of garden work.

Below and **right:** *Instead of traditional borders, if you have a gravel bed like this one, plant through the gravel. It will make a more pleasing background than bare soil.*

Alternatives to borders

Your bed could form a wedge shape in the front garden, widest by the pavement and narrowest near the building, thus offering space for big plants as well as small. Or you could make the whole of your front garden into one huge bed, with the main path to the door running around the edge. If it's too large for this, introduce a few stepping-stone paths through it so that you can explore the bed more easily.

The delights of gravel have been described on pages 36-38. You can expand on this theme by planting a variety of plants of all sizes directly through the gravel, rather as you might plant in a traditional border. With no defined edge, it will give the impression of a garden where plants come first and the landscaping is a setting for them.

Make the plants work

As important as the shape or size of a border are the plants you put in it. The basic rules — such as planting the tallest at the back with the carpeters at the front, and the principles of using harmonising or contrasting colours — apply whatever the size of garden, but there must be enough framework plants to give the garden structure (and maybe necessary screening) throughout the year.

A garden with too many evergreens will be predictable and probably unexciting, but to avoid bare patches where the small garden is exposed with all its boundaries and buildings it's necessary to include enough evergreens to screen the worst views and to give a sense of growth

throughout the year. Although there can be no rigid rules, it's worth aiming to have at least a quarter of your plants evergreen — which is not as boring as it sounds, since there are evergold, evergrey and ever-variegated plants within this heading.

There are also evergreen non-woody plants, such as bergenias and ajugas (bugles), as well as a number of sedges and grasses.

Evergreen ground-cover plants, such as ivy and *Pachysandra terminalis*, are useful because they give 'texture' to the garden as well as a little year-round colour.

Make full use of multi-merit shrubs, such as the dogwoods with their attractive summer foliage, autumn colour when the leaves fall, and colourful

winter stems. *Cornus alba* 'Sibirica' is a good one to start with.

Use plenty of evergreens with attractive flowers too, such as hebes and cistus (though these are both likely to be vulnerable in very cold or exposed regions).

Pack in plenty of bulbs. Within the same piece of ground you can often accommodate spring-flowering and autumn-flowering kinds, and perhaps even some for the summer too. If you choose types that multiply and flower freely if left to their own

Cornus alba *'Sibirica' is the type of multi-merit shrub well worth growing in a small garden. It should not grow too tall, and it has good autumn colour followed by bright red winter stems. You can see a suggestion of both in this photograph.*

Be sure to include a few shrubs that bring late interest to your borders. Ceratostigma plumbaginoides *remains compact, flowers late and has the bonus of good autumn colour.*

devices, like daffodils, camass-ias and colchicums, the show

will be better year-on-year without the cost of regular replanting.

It's always worth including a few shrubs with good autumn colour, such as *Ceratostigma plumbaginoides*. Some of the best-known autumn-colour trees may be too large for a small garden, but some small trees have good autumn colour too — try *Prunus* 'Kansan' or *Malus* 'John Downie' if you want small trees that look good in spring as well as

autumn. The various amelan-chiers can be grown as shrubs or trees, and their fine autumn colour is a bonus after the masses of white spring flowers.

It's not practical to have more than a few pockets of autumn foliage colour in a limited space, so be sure to include some autumn-flowering plants in your borders. Some dwarf chrysanthemums flower late, and the beautiful Guernsey lily (*Nerine bowdenii*) will often flower well into the winter.

Plant to create pockets of colour that extend the season as much as possible. This picture of Nerine bowdenii *was taken in December! You must find space for a clump of something as good as this.*

Patio pleasure

The most natural position for a patio is adjoining the house, perhaps next to patio doors or French windows. This makes it a more integral part of the house, and meals and entertaining are that much more convenient if you can simply step out onto your patio without negotiating garden paths.

However, such a position may not be ideal in a small garden. If your back garden gets the sun only in the early morning or late afternoon, it may appear gloomy for the greater part of the day. Shade is more of a problem with a house than a bungalow because of the greater height of the walls.

If you are fortunate enough to have a reasonably large side garden, consider placing the patio on one corner of the house, perhaps set at 45 degrees if your overall garden design is also based on a grid set at an angle to the building. Provided the aspects are appropriate, you will have more hours of sunshine to enjoy.

If your side garden is narrow, however, a corner site will probably be inappropriate, especially as it could be positioned in a wind tunnel between two buildings.

In a long and narrow garden it may be possible to position the patio along one side. This could provide a useful visual break and mark the point

Below: *A patio set at an angle to the house can look more interesting, and mixing paving materials also adds style.*

where the garden has a change in style and another 'room' is entered.

The only other practical position, if the garden is short, is the end of the back garden. This sounds unpromising, but does have its advantages. If there is a tall hedge or wall behind, it may be a more private position if you are overlooked by other houses opposite. You will look back towards your own home, of course, but if you make good

To enclose or not ...

A patio can be enclosed with tall screen-block walls on some of the sides, or low raised beds planted with flowers. You can further give it a sense of enclosure by using overhead beams. These look best set into the house wall, as they make it seem very much like an outdoor room; or you can build a free-standing patio overhead made from beams supported on stout posts or pillars.

A patio overhead provides a useful sense of structure, but if the garden is really small it may make it seem even smaller, especially if you clothe it with vigorous climbers. Climbers are admittedly useful to provide shade, but bear in mind that they also cast shade that other plants may not appreciate, and they can drip annoyingly after a shower of rain!

Paving in proportion

If you make a traditional paved patio, take care that it doesn't look bleak and boring. An expanse of paving can often be accommodated in a large garden because the harshness of texture is diluted by the larger ratio of plants and lawn to paved area. Where space is restricted there's a risk that the paving can look out of proportion to the planted area.

If the garden is really tiny — or if it's a courtyard or basement garden — then the answer may be to pave it all

use of wall shrubs to soften the walls this needn't be an unattractive prospect.

If you set your patio at an angle across a corner at the end of the garden, and use a few suitable screening shrubs, or perhaps a screen-block wall, you may be able to look across the garden at an angle and avoid most buildings in your line of sight. This could also be a very private position.

A patio placed at the end of the garden or to one side will

Overhead beams linking the building to an area of paving help to tie garden and house together visually.

provide a useful focal point, and the path leading to it will have a clear purpose. Avoid placing your patio too far from the house, however, otherwise you will be less inclined to use it for eating and entertaining.

Plenty of plants in containers will help to soften the potential harshness of a paved area, but bear in mind that they all require watering — daily in summer! This is a corner of the author's garden where shrubs and small trees are grown in containers to give the garden a sense of maturity as well as to provide additional privacy.

around the patio, spaces provided by leaving out the occasional paving slab, containers, or — best of all — a combination of different planting spaces.

Container problems

Beware of depending too heavily on containers. They can look superb for a few months in summer when packed with colourful summer flowers, but plain unattractive for the winter months. Even if you plant plenty of spring-flowering bulbs and spring flowers such as forget-me-nots and wallflowers, containers will inevitably look stark and unclothed for many months.

Use a few large containers for permanent evergreen shrubs, but where possible leave space in and around your patio where plants can be set into the ground. A dormant clematis in a container will look depressingly like a dead plant, yet planted in the ground near to the wall where a paving slab would have been, it will hardly be noticed until it bursts into leaf and bloom again.

It is also easier to hide bare soil with a ground-cover plant than it is to hide bare soil in a container. Using a decorative mulch such as chipped bark will improve things a little, but you will still be aware of the container and the fact that it looks bleak and uncolourful.

Another reason to beware of too many containers is the need to water them, unless

and not apologise for it. You can work wonders with plants in containers, and you can even have patio ponds, and ornaments, and perhaps garden lighting, which can give it all the vibrant impact that you could desire.

If the garden is small but too large to be paved in its entirety, then build in plenty of planting space. This can consist of raised beds on or you are prepared to install an automatic watering system. Even if you are willing to spend considerable time watering *every* day during the warm months, there will be a time when you want to go away for a few days. Even helpful neighbours may not be enthusiastic if there are too many containers to water.

Enhancing your patio

Try incorporating some low raised beds around one or two sides of a formal patio, and if there's space it's worth introducing a raised bed as a feature within it.

If possible, offset a large area of paving with a vertical element. This can be structural, like the posts or columns for a patio overhead, or organic — an evergreen wall shrub such

Try to clothe the walls of your patio, but don't choose very vigorous climbers. Large-flowered clematis are always a safe choice. This one is 'Bagatelle'.

as pyracantha, a climber such as an ivy, or even a small tree in a large pot or tub. A laburnum will remain compact in a large patio pot, yet at perhaps 8 ft (2.4 m) or more in height it will make your patio more verdant and will help to integrate it into the rest of the garden.

Using the walls

Most patios are constructed next to the house for reasons already discussed. One of the

drawbacks is the dominance of walls, whether the house walls or screen walls that you construct for privacy. If they remain undecorated or unclothed they are likely to appear oppressive and may make the patio look gloomy rather than bright and cheerful. So think carefully about

Too much paving can be off-putting. A few raised beds will usually improve it radically.

how patio walls can be improved.

Climbers are an obvious choice, but avoid very rampant ones like *Parthenocissus,* which includes Virginia creeper and Boston ivy. Even ordinary ivy is unsuitable unless you choose a variegated small-leaved variety that's slow-growing.

Concentrate on climbers with scent, such as summer jasmines (*Jasminum officinale*) and honeysuckles — though use the latter only if you are prepared to keep them pruned, otherwise they will take up too much space, even tumbling back down on themselves from the top of the support and so obtruding into the sitting area even further.

Flowering climbers that are not too vigorous, such as large-flowered hybrid clematis or climbing roses, will bring beauty without taking up too much space. But don't use roses in a position where their thorns would be liable to prick someone.

Wall shrubs that can be trained and clipped to a flat profile are particularly useful; examples include pyracanthas and the fishbone cotoneaster (*C. horizontalis*). Another common shrub worth considering is *Euonymus fortunei* in its variegated varieties such as 'Emerald Gaiety'. Although *E.*

fortunei is normally seen as a prostrate ground-hugger, the stems will grow vertically if planted against a wall. As the growth is never too thick and bushy and it isn't over-vigorous, an occasional trim with secateurs is all it needs.

A word of warning: if you have a phobia about spiders, you may want to avoid climbers and wall shrubs close you where you sit and perhaps eat. Beware of bees and wasps too when pyracanthas are in flower.

Pyracanthas are a good choice to plant against the house wall, giving attractive flowers in summer and berries in autumn.

Other sitting areas

An arbour adds that something special to a garden, where you can sit in seclusion.

Patios are popular because they provide a paved area where you can sit and enjoy your garden on warm and pleasant days. But there are other ways of providing somewhere pleasant to sit that may have even more appeal in a small garden. In dry weather a hard-wearing lawn will do just as well, though you may feel a little exposed.

Add an arbour

An arbour, with a cosy seat, will make a charming feature and it can look just as pleasing

If it's difficult to find a suitable position for a patio, consider a summerhouse, which can help to provide a degree of privacy as well as useful shelter.

in a small town garden as in a large country cottage garden.

A waterproof bench seat is usually built into the arbour, but that doesn't mean it has to

be hard to sit on or drab to look at. Use plenty of colourful cushions — you will linger for longer and they will become a short-term focal point.

Summerhouses

An attractive summerhouse (provided it is large enough) will provide sheltered space for sitting, and even a balcony with some models. There are many bright and sunny days in spring and autumn when it's too cold or windy to sit on an exposed patio but when a summerhouse provides all the shelter you need. As a summerhouse has a back, and sometimes enclosed sides, you are almost guaranteed a sense of privacy if you position it appropriately, and the roof

51

prevents you being overlooked from the upstairs windows of adjoining properties.

Some summerhouses are highly decorative and can be a focal point in their own right. Consider whether in your garden a summerhouse might be a better option than a patio in terms of visual appeal and the best use of space. You can always pave an area in front of it to make a combined patio/summerhouse area.

Teahouse

If a summerhouse doesn't appeal, then maybe a teahouse will. If you create a Japanese-style garden, a teahouse will look far more appropriate than a summerhouse. The front may be open but the sides and back provide that essential protection from cold winds, so you will still be able to use it extensively in spring and autumn as well as the summer months.

You will probably have to build this kind of structure yourself to fit the space available, but it's not too difficult — you can use something simple yet striking for the walls, like the rolls of tied reed that can sometimes be bought.

A teahouse, like this one built from scratch by Trevor Crisp, could provide a comfortable sitting spot from which to enjoy your garden.

Ways with water

Water-gardening enthusiasts will usually find a way to incorporate one or more ponds into their garden. If your interest lies in fish more than plants, it may be the dominant feature, but bear in mind that a pond in winter can emphasise the greyness and bleakness of those cold days. If you are interested in giving your garden year-round appeal, then keep water features in proportion … like the paved areas.

This part-sunk, part-raised pond in the patio area is a constant source of fascination and pleasure. Here a datura (now more correctly brugmansia) adds an exotic touch.

This 'stream' in part of the author's garden became rather overgrown once the plants settled down. As so much wildlife was attracted by the dense vegetation and water, it was turned into a bog garden.

Ponds and streams

Generally it's best to have a formal style of pond linked in some way with the patio. It does not have to form part of it, but could perhaps adjoin it. Having your pond in a highly visible position will give you hours of pleasure. And the formal shape (usually rectangular, circular or semi-circular) looks less incongruous than attempts at integrating an informal pond.

It *is* possible to build a natural-looking pond or stream in a small garden, but if your garden is very tiny the difficulties will be considerable.

It may be possible to build a meandering 'stream' along one side of the garden, offering plenty of scope for pondside planting. You can have pond

53

liners made to almost any shape and size, including long and narrow.

Small informally-shaped pools can be tucked into flower beds (avoid overhanging trees if possible). Some shade won't matter if you want it primarily as a wildlife pond, but flowering pond plants such as waterlilies need plenty of sunlight to flower well.

If you just want somewhere for frogs to spawn and birds to drink, a small pool made from an old half-barrel sunk almost to its rim into the edge of a border will be inconspicuous yet will attract plenty of wildlife.

Ponds need to have a reasonably large surface area to achieve a satisfactory biological balance with clear water for most of the time, and they also need a large enough volume to support a small collection of healthy fish. If you want to stock the pond heavily or include demanding fish like koi or orfe, you will need an efficient in-pond biological filter suitable for small ponds. Avoid the type that requires you to accommodate an unattractive black box outside the pond, which would be particularly conspicuous in a small garden.

Consider a raised patio pond. You don't even have to build it yourself, as there are now plenty of preformed raised patio ponds that you simply assemble and fill with water! Many of them include a small cascade or fountain so that you can bring the magic of the movement and sound of running water into your garden.

Fountains

Bubble and pebble fountains, where the water gurgles or springs from a bed of pebbles, will bring any corner of the garden to life. You can make them yourself or buy them as a kit. A drilled boulder, where water emerges through a drilled rock to flow back to a reservoir hidden beneath pebbles, is another focal-point water feature that brings the sight and sound of water with minimal risk to small children. Features like this are ideal for small-scale gardens.

Wall fountains come in many styles, from the classic reconstituted stone lion masks to clean-line resin modern all-in-one units complete with built-in pump. There is bound to be

There's always room for a wall fountain, and it will give you the sight and sound of running water if you don't have space for a pond.

one to suit your style of gardening and individual taste — not to mention pocket.

Wall fountains are best on a patio or house wall, and for practical reasons the nearer they are to a power supply the quicker and cheaper they will be to install. Sometimes, however, it's worth installing one at the end of the garden if there is a suitable wall, to act as a focal point and to encourage exploration of the garden. As the water is recycled (from a reservoir in the ground or a dish if it is a self-contained unit), you need only take into account the power supply.

This simple water feature was made in a dustbin lid in less than an hour, to bring interest to a dull corner of the garden.

Containers — a movable feast

While no garden seems complete without a few ornaments and plants in containers, they assume a more important role in small gardens. Apart from their own intrinsic merits, their mobility is invaluable in ringing the changes. No matter how well designed and planted, a small garden inevitably runs the risk of becoming predictable and even boring after a while. Anything that you can replant seasonally (or within the season), and any ornament light enough to be moved around, will ensure that there is always something different to stimulate interest.

Where to use them

Containers can be used freely all around the garden, but bear in mind that they will all require watering. It makes sense to restrict the number of containers to those you feel happy to water and feed frequently (and this means at least once a day during the warm months of summer). Containers filled with half-dead or starved and stunted plants will draw attention for the wrong reasons.

If your time is limited and you don't have an automatic watering system, it makes sense to keep most of your

Above: *Grouping plants close to the door makes watering easier, and also adds interest to what could be a boring part of the garden. Here ordinary rhubarb is being used as a foliage plant!*

containers close to the back or front door. Even if you use a hose for watering, it's a chore to have to keep dragging it around the garden.

Another good reason to use some containers by the front door is that this always creates a good impression, especially if the flowers are fragrant, or just

A few plants in containers by the front door helps to give the impression of a warm welcome.

Although large ones are heavy and difficult to move, you can reposition them more easily than a windowbox or a hanging basket. Heavy containers can be moved around on rollers or on a garden trolley if you can enlist help in lifting them on and off.

Use containers with plants in full bloom as focal points around the garden. Ornamental pots and tubs are best for permanent plants, such as shrubs, as they will have an intrinsic decorative merit when the plants they contain are in an 'off' season. There's not much point in spending a lot of money on a high-quality ornamental container if it is to be hidden by trailing plants and bushy summer flowers.

Groups of containers are almost always more pleasing than individual pots. By placing smaller ones in front of larger ones, the bases of plain and uninteresting pots will be masked by other plants, and the whole group will make more of a 'splash'. This is important if you want them to make a focal point.

Small basement gardens or any small garden with walls to

colourful in winter. Clipped bays or potted topiary will add a touch of class, even to a town house with a minimal front garden.

If you don't have space for seasonal bedding plants because the main garden has been planted with permanent inhabitants, use windowboxes, tubs and troughs to grow all those colourful flowers that you would otherwise miss out on. It's important to have some pockets of colour and plants that change from season to season.

Tubs and large pots can be ornamental in their own right, but even a plain pot or an old half-barrel can become a focal point with a stunning plant.

Windowboxes

Windowboxes will certainly enhance your home, and if you can arrange matching boxes beneath both upstairs and downstairs windows the impact will be that much greater. The planting doesn't have to be complicated: stunning effects can be created using just one type of plant. The cascading geraniums (*Pelargonium*) popular in some Continental countries are always admired, and the easy busy lizzie (*Impatiens*) and trailing petunias such as those great performers the Surfinias, will flower for the whole summer and look good from a distance as well as close to.

Fibrous-rooted begonias (*Begonia semperflorens* varieties) also flower summer-long, but they are generally too compact to make a show from the ground if used in an upstairs windowbox.

'Continental' cascade pelargoniums are excellent for windowboxes, but you could also create a matching tower like this.

A group of containers like this will be a real focal point within the garden.

ful one, and weaknesses are very visible.

Having a supply of replacement plants is the best way to overcome the problem. In the case of spring-flowering bulbs, it pays to grow plenty of small bulbs in pots so that when they bloom you can plunge the pots (or simply knock the plants out of the pots) in windowboxes or other containers to replace those going over. With summer-flowering plants, it's worth having a succession of summer flowers growing on in boxes small enough to be slipped into the outer display windowbox. As the contents of

clothe can be made more interesting with lots of windowboxes and half-baskets … but don't set them in regimented rows. Try staggering them to spread the cover.

Painting the wall white or another pale colour will throw more light into what may be a gloomy area, and is likely to show off the plants to better advantage. As windowboxes and half-baskets can be lifted off their brackets and supports, painting the wall periodically should not be a problem.

Lining up beauty
Although some summer bedding plants will bloom and look beautiful for months, many other useful container plants have a more limited season. Spring displays of bulbs are also often disap-

pointingly short-lived. In a garden where everything has to look good because everything is on show, you don't want windowboxes that *have* looked good. In a small garden, a tatty windowbox will be as conspicuous as a beauti-

Keep the colour coming in winter and early spring by adding a few plants bought as they are coming into flower.

one begin to look tatty, remove the liner and replace it with one full of flowers at their prime.

This kind of intensive use for containers is possible on a small scale even though it might be impractical for a large garden.

Hanging baskets

Traditionally, hanging baskets are suspended on brackets from the house wall, but in this position a large half-basket may be just as effective. And you don't have to keep turning it round to ensure even growth.

Try hanging baskets from a patio overhead or even from the side beams of a pergola.

If you choose appropriate plants, a hanging basket suspended from the branch of a tree can add a touch of the unusual, but bear in mind that many plants will resent the amount of shade they receive in this position. Go for shade-tolerant plants such as busy lizzies, with small-leaved ivies if you want something to trail over the edge. Don't assume these baskets will receive enough water when it rains, as the tree foliage will deflect most of what falls.

Winter colour

It isn't practical to fill all your containers with winter-interest plants; many of them will have been refilled with spring bedding plants and bulbs. But do set a few aside to plant up for winter colour.

For tubs, troughs and windowboxes you will have to depend on young specimens of hardy shrubs, such as skimmias and gaultherias, which

Try hanging baskets in some less usual spots. This one is hanging by the garden shed, and the ribbon adds another nice touch.

This winter-interest trough, photographed in January, contains hellebores, Carex morrowii *'Evergold',* Euphorbia amygdaloides *'Purpurea', and* Ajuga reptans *'Catlin's Giant'.*

'Disposable' plants

It's worth spending a bit on 'disposable' plants if you can afford it — plants that you know will be killed by the cold and have to be discarded … but not before you've had a few weeks of unseasonal colour!

Cape heathers (*Erica hiemalis* and *E. gracilis*) or even year-round pot chrysanthemums can be used, and the Christmas cherries (*Solanum capsicastrum* and *S. pseudocapsicum*), with their attractive orange-red fruits, should give several weeks of colour and cheer before having to be discarded.

have long-lasting berries, and small variegated shrubs like *Euonymus fortunei* 'Emerald 'n' Gold' or 'Emerald Gaiety'. For trailers the tough small-leaved variegated ivies are invaluable.

Don't ignore evergreen border plants, either. The number of these is limited, but there are some common ones that you should make use of. The various varieties of *Ajuga reptans*, most of which are attractively variegated, make interesting plants for the edge of a container, while there are colourful evergreen grasses and sedges such as *Carex morrowii* 'Evergold'.

Try to add a few Christmas roses (*Helleborus niger*) or Lenten roses (*H. orientalis*), as a few flowers are always appreciated. Buy some pots of early-flowering bulbs such as snowdrops and *Iris danfordiae*, and squeeze these in between the shrubs. When they've finished,

take them out and replace them with something else coming into flower (winter pansies or *Iris reticulata*, perhaps). Pots of plants like these just coming into flower are available from most garden centres.

This late-autumn and early-winter trough contains Cape heathers and ornamental cabbages.

Opposite: *Ornaments and pieces of garden art give you the chance to express your personality! This abstract ornament is in The Garden in Mind, at Stansted Park, Sussex.*

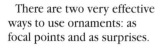

Focus on ornaments

Ornaments serve a similar purpose in the garden to their role in the home. They add interest to otherwise dull corners, or act as a focal point to draw the eye. They also tell you a lot about the owner. To one person a garden gnome is the height of bad taste, to another it adds that touch of fun that a garden needs. You can use a classical bust in an alcove, or go to the other extreme and use an abstract and perhaps outrageous piece (such as a pair of legs sticking out of the lawn) to show that you have your own strongly developed individual sense of artistic qualities.

Some fortunate gardeners would only consider displaying a genuine antique urn or vase; others are happy with a repro-duction made from reconstitut-ed stone at a fraction of the cost.

The best advice is to use ornaments that please *you*, for if you worry about what other people think you will never be satisfied … there will always be other gardeners with different views.

There are two very effective ways to use ornaments: as focal points and as surprises.

Focal points

An obelisk can be a focal point on a large estate, while a bust on a plinth or perhaps a large sculpture serves the same purpose in a large garden. In a small garden the ornaments have to be scaled down in proportion. Anything too grandiose will look out of place — it's prudent to avoid a pair of rampant lions guarding the gate of a small semi-detached house on a modern housing estate, or a large naked lady in the centre of your back lawn. The threshold of appropriate taste for the setting will have been crossed.

In a large garden you can use ornaments lavishly as focal points with little risk of one clashing with another. But if you cram too many into a small area they will lose their impact as focal points. A good rule of thumb is not to have two conspicuous ornaments in eyeshot at the same time.

That's not as limiting as it sounds. A well-designed small garden will not all be taken in 'at a glance'. There should be areas to explore, different views around a large shrub or a trellis, and yet another view from the patio or arbour. A focal-point ornament that is behind you as you stand at one side of the garden will be in front when you're at the other side.

This traditional ornament makes a particularly good focal point because the golden shrub behind lifts it from the background.

Be bold in your design

It takes courage to be bold in design and to use garden ornaments in an adventurous or unexpected way.

But it's worth the risk — the effect can be to make a small garden appear very special and to make your visitors take note.

When the 'what and why' questions start, you know you've been sufficiently bold!

Ornaments don't have to be high or big to be effective: a matching pair of stone doves on the lawn can have as much impact as a sundial (and in a shady area will look far more appropriate).

A sundial or a large ornament on a plinth cannot easily be moved around, but the 'doves' could be moved to a different position on the lawn say once a week to make the garden a little less predictable.

Left: *This cat strikes a realistic pose.*

Below: *These birds seem very happy among the chamomile.*

Surprises

Surprise ornaments are most effective if *not* instantly visible. Half the pleasure is in discovering them.

The easiest kind of 'surprise' ornaments are animal figures placed among plants — particularly foliage plants. The scene changes as the plants grow, and again the ornaments can be moved around the garden to create different plant/ornament combinations.

Who could fail to pause to admire this figure of a young boy coming out of the bushes?

Who could fail to pause to admire this figure of a young boy coming out of the bushes?

Frogs sitting at the pond's edge are a popular choice, but they will probably look more impressive if discovered sitting among the vegetation at the side of the pond, or even sitting in the water.

Don't necessarily confine yourself to animal figures. The crouching figure of a small boy, for example, can be a delight when discovered emerging from between attractive foliage shrubs.

If you want to be adventurous, use a small dragon figure tucked in among herbs that someone will bend down to pick or smell ... They will be surprised (and hopefully delighted) to discover such an unusual creature lurking among the leaves.

You can use these small-scale surprise ornaments lavishly in a small garden. And if necessary you can put some away for a while and replace them with others, then rotate them again in another season.

Garden art

If ornaments aren't your thing, why not set about creating an impact in a less conventional way?

Paint a large white solid circle on your wall or fence, then wait for the questions. For no matter how tatty the fence or unpromising the wall, it will suddenly have become a talking-point. Then, when you use your white circle to frame the head of a standard rose in full flower, or maybe the stunning blooms of a pot-grown *Strelitzia* (bird-of-paradise flower) or the blue spikes of a tub of camassias, the compliments will begin to flow.

If you have artistic ability, don't hesitate to paint a scene on an otherwise boring wall in an unpromising position. You don't have to be elaborate or make it fussy — a plain background with painted sprigs of ivy, and perhaps an artistic

This plain fence does nothing to enhance the flowers. But you can work a little magic with a white circle (see next page) ...

... The white circle (cut out from a piece of expanded polystyrene for easy removal later) frames the rose and transforms the scene.

Illuminating that attractive tree at the end of the garden with a floodlight might look good from your viewpoint, but if there's a house opposite, the glare of the light may not be so welcome there. A good general rule for a small garden is to position the light high but point the beam low, rather than having a low-level light directed upwards.

Powerful mains lights are useful for security lighting and floodlighting in large gardens, but in a small area very bright beams are inappropriate, and low-voltage lights are adequate for most lighting effects.

Low-voltage systems have other benefits. They run off a transformer plugged into the mains indoors, so, unlike mains lighting, they do not require skilled or expensive wiring-in by a professional electrician. They are also more mobile — mains lighting circuits have to be fixed fairly close to where you expect to use the lights. It's much easier to move low-voltage systems around the garden to suit the season and the effect or mood you want to create. This mobility is important if you want to squeeze every last ounce of pleasure from a small garden. You must make the available

space work by appearing in as many different lights (literally and figuratively) as possible.

Try moving the lights around to highlight different beds as each one is at its best, or simply pick out one or two really striking plants — perhaps a red-hot poker (kniphofia) or a phormium. Don't dismiss white flowers, which show up particularly well when illuminated.

During the winter months there will be few flowers to experiment with, but there will still be plenty of opportunities to explore the potential of garden lights if you use a little

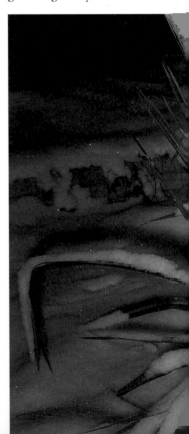

impression of a flower such as a clematis, is sufficient to create a very individual effect.

Throwing light on the problem

Garden lights are another worthwhile investment, not only because they will provide more hours of pleasure from your garden, but also because you can use them to highlight different facets of the garden by moving them around. This is another way to compensate for the restrictions that come with a small garden.

Anyone who has used garden lights already will need no convincing that they're a good idea. But the smaller the garden, the more carefully they have to be used.

imagination. Ornaments shout out for attention. Whether a key focal point or an almost hidden ornament, it will be as striking by night as by day ... if you remember to use your lights creatively.

Some gardeners try to use light to create a daytime effect and regard shadows and dark areas as a failure, but this approach is unwise. Most low-powered garden lights have a small area of illumination (an advantage rather than a draw-back where there are neigh-bours to consider), and spot-lights will emphasise the large area of unlit garden.

Don't worry about shadows: they can add to the sense of drama, and can play an impor-tant role with ornaments. It may be possible to cast dram-atic shadows of the piece onto a wall behind, or in the case of a plant create a moving pattern as the shadows dance in a breeze.

Lights have another immense benefit in a small garden: they are selective in what they help you to see. They pick out the good points within the garden, and should leave things like your neighbour's garden shed, the fence at the end of the garden, or those surrounding

houses, lost in the darkness. Your garden may be tiny, but if the lights illuminate only the best of your garden, nobody will be conscious of the limitations.

Solar nightlights
How can you have a nightlight powered by the sun? This apparent contra-diction is achieved by solar cells storing the energy of sunlight during the day and using it to power the lights at night. Some of these lights have an optional standby battery system so that your party event is not a disaster if it's been too gloomy that day for the sun to generate enough power.

These are not an ideal solution for all your garden lighting problems, but they are particularly advanta-geous if you want to move your lights around a lot without worrying about cables (these should *never* trail across paths, for exam-ple, even if the system is low-voltage). They are also very useful where there is no convenient power-point from which to run a low-voltage system.

Don't put the garden lights away for the winter. There are many dramatic scenes to be illuminated, like this phormium in the snow.

Growing to eat

This is an area of potential conflict. Not only between members of your family, but also within your own mind if you're a keen gardener *and* appreciate the delights of fresh produce for the kitchen.

Small gardens usually need all the available space simply to fit in the flowers and other ornamentals. And even if you are prepared to relinquish some of that precious space for the cooking pot, it's difficult to hide a vegetable plot as you might in a larger garden. Unless you treat the problem with thought and sensitivity, the 'edible' garden will impinge very visibly on the ornamental.

That doesn't mean ornamental and culinary can't co-exist, it just means careful planning and realistic expectations. You won't easily feed a family of four from a few windowboxes and patio tubs planted with vegetables, or be self-sufficient in fruit the year round. But you can enjoy 'treats' to supplement the fruit and vegetables that you have to buy, and you may be able to be self-sufficient in herbs (depending on how many you use).

Your garden fence can be laden with fruit like this in autumn, and the spring blossom is also attractive. This is an espalier pear, but cordons are also suitable.

ornamentals anyway. If you're really keen on herbs, why not make a herb garden? Unlike most vegetable plots, herb gardens can be very attractive ornamental features, bringing their own strong design element.

Here, rhubarb is being grown in a container alongside Chlorophytum comosum *and busy lizzie in a shady porch.*

Finding space

If you can partition an area off for the kitchen garden, this is ideal ... provided that most of it is in full sun for at least half the day. A few crops can be grown in a shady position, such as spinach and rhubarb, but don't expect tight cabbage heads, good Brussels sprouts or luscious ripe peaches in a spot that receives little sun.

Screening the area with a trellis is better than using a hedge or a solid fence, as it should let through a little more light. You can always grow a blackberry or hybrid berry along it, provided that you prune and train it methodically.

Fruit is perhaps best integrated as part of the ornamental garden. You can't do this easily with a row of raspberries, but there's plenty of scope for many other fruits. Make the most of trained fruit such as cordons and espaliers, both of which are space-saving. You can even grow a few fruit trees (including apples and peaches) in pots or tubs on your patio!

A few vegetables can be grown among the flowers — in a potager garden (where flowers and vegetables are grown together in the same specially created beds) if you are adventurous enough to make one, or in flower borders otherwise. Some are ornamental enough to be grown for their decorative value anyway (see pages 69–70). Otherwise, grow suitable vegetables in containers of various kinds.

Most herbs are easy to accommodate in an ornamental garden — some are grown as

Economising

There is not much point in spending twice as much on growing vegetables in containers as you could buy them for in the shops. If you buy new containers, good potting compost and maybe fertilisers too, the economics become dubious.

To cut down on cost, use growing bags for more than one crop. Use them new for a high-value 'hungry' crop such as tomatoes or cucumbers, then for a less demanding crop such as lettuces (you will still have to feed them). After that, mix the contents of the bag with an equal part of garden soil, plus added fertiliser, to use in pots and containers.

Vegetables

It's not the growing of vegetables in a small garden that's the problem, it's deciding the point at which it's *worth* giving up valuable space to them. There's not much point attempting to grow maincrop potatoes in a small space — you will end up devoting most of your garden to a crop you can buy cheaply and for a lot less effort. On the other hand,

It's worth growing a few tubers of a very early variety of potato in a container started off indoors. New potatoes are worth the effort!

Above right: *'Dunluce' in a growing bag* **Below:** *Harvesting 'Maris Bard' from a pot*

a few pots or growing bags of a very early variety will provide you with a real treat at a time when 'new' potatoes are expensive. You must, of course, be prepared to protect them from frost.

Using containers

Many vegetables can be grown in containers such as large pots, growing bags, and even in windowboxes.

Root crops should be a low priority: although turnips, carrots and onions can be grown in containers, the yield for a given area is low, so this is probably not the best use of limited space. If you really want to rise to the challenge, choose varieties with small roots, such as round-rooted forcing carrots, or beet that responds well to close spacing by producing succulent 'baby beet'. Grow spring onions rather than bulbing onions, then you'll have an early and worthwhile crop for the space devoted to them.

Peas and dwarf **French beans** will usually provide a few reasonable pickings if grown in a growing bag or large pot. Bear in mind that

Tomato 'Totem' cropping well in a 10 in (25 cm) pot

peas will require staking, so choose a very dwarf variety.

A reasonable crop of self-blanching **celery** can be obtained from a growing bag, but you may prefer to concentrate your efforts on more valuable crops that will yield over a long period, such as bush **cucumbers** or **courgettes**. Both of these can be really successful.

The most popular choice remains **tomatoes**, and most varieties will do well in growing bags. 'Totem' and other very dumpy varieties will produce an impressive yield from a 10 in (25 cm) pot without the need for elaborate supports. They will do just as well in a large windowbox, and you can also grow trailers like 'Tumbler' in a hanging basket as well as a windowbox. Whether you would rather have tomatoes in your hanging baskets than a ball of colourful flowers, only you can decide!

Lettuces are really easy crops to grow in containers, giving a quick crop with reasonable value for the space. Ordinary hearting varieties are fine for growing bags and other containers in non-decorative areas, but if you are growing them in a windowbox choose a cut-and-come-again non-hearting variety like 'Salad Bowl'. That way the container will still look attractive after harvesting a meal or two, whereas ordinary hearting varieties will leave very unattractive gaps after you've cut them. 'Red Salad Bowl' makes a nice variation, and you could even try alternate plants of the green and red varieties.

In the border

Growing vegetables among flowers in the border can be successful if you get the balance right and choose those that look decorative. Though some gardeners are prepared to plant **cabbages** and **cauliflowers** in their flower borders, most of us would probably find this an unacceptable use of valuable space in a small area where visual impact is important.

Runner beans make excellent back-of-border plants, and they can even be used to cover a trellis. In some countries they are grown primarily as ornamentals, so they justify a place with the flowers, perhaps grown up a wigwam of canes. If you prefer **French beans** to runner beans, grow climbing French varieties.

Vegetables with ornamental foliage also look good in a mixed border. Beetroot and Swiss chard are two of the best examples. **Beetroot** have very ornamental purple-red foliage, and there are varieties grown primarily as decorative foliage plants. Sow them in groups or clusters rather than in rows, and thin out a few roots to eat as they become larger. Leave most of them to reach full size

Not everyone is keen on rhubarb chard as a vegetable, but you can grow it as an ornamental instead. Here it's seen as a centrepiece to a half-barrel display, surrounded by lobelia.

Lettuces look good among the flowers, the non-hearting varieties like 'Salad Bowl' more so than hearting varieties (see page 69).

Even a few **tomato** plants won't look amiss, especially if you choose a bush variety with small fruits such as 'Red Alert'. These do not require tall stakes, and the small red fruits look very decorative. Unless you have a large family, you will be able to harvest enough to eat and still leave the plant looking decorative.

without becoming over-large or tough, to maintain the display for as long as possible.

Swiss chard has large, bright red leaves, so decorative that the plant is sometimes grown among summer bedding plants purely for its decorative appeal. Harvest just a few leaves at a time from each plant so that you don't spoil the display prematurely.

Carrots, with their feathery green foliage, also make a good foil for bright flowers. Eat some of the thinnings, but leave most of the plants to reach full size — you'll have a heavier crop, and the decorative display won't be cut short.

Fruit

Apples and **pears** are ideal for training as cordons along a sunny fence or wall. These can be really decorative and take up so little space that there's room for one or two in almost every garden. Fans are very decorative too (and you can have fan cherries and peaches as well as apples), but they do take up much more space.

You can use espaliers as internal dividers within the garden, but they also make decorative fruit 'trees' to grow against a wall or fence.

Beware of full-sized fruit trees in a small garden, though bush apples on a very dwarfing rootstock should be satisfactory (look for the label M27 rootstock or ask your garden centre or nursery to recommend one suitable for a small garden).

The so-called 'flagpole' apple tree varieties, which grow pillar-like, take up no more ground-space than a medium-sized shrub, yet they can yield a whole column of fruit, which are produced naturally on short spurs off the main stem rather than from long horizontal branches.

Fruit in pots and tubs hardly sounds worthwhile, but if you only have a balcony or basement garden, or maybe want a decorative fruiting feature for your patio, pot-grown fruits are a possibility. Don't expect a heavy crop, however, and consider how much regular watering and feeding will be necessary in order to obtain a crop at all! You can't always measure these things in financial cost, or in time and effort expended, however. The opportunity to pick your own apples from the patio (or even a peach from its pot) may outweigh all the practical problems.

This apple 'Jester' has an M27 rootstock. It's very important to choose an appropriate rootstock for fruit to be used in a small garden.

Apples in pots should be a low priority, because you can grow them in a limited space as flagpoles or decorative espaliers. **Peaches**, on the other hand, are worthy of consideration as a pot fruit. The blossom is beautiful, and you can move the plant into a greenhouse or conservatory when it needs an early start or a bit of extra warmth and protection.

Growing soft-fruit bushes such as gooseberries, blackcurrants and redcurrants in containers will take up a lot of space and time, but if you enjoy a few freshly-picked gooseberries or redcurrants straight from the bush, don't be deterred. You will get a respectable crop, but you are unlikely to have space for more than one or two bushes in containers.

Gooseberries can be grown as attractive cordons against a fence, requiring much less watering and feeding.

Strawberries are understandably popular fruits for a small garden. They take up *relatively* little space (but for a given weight of crop they may not be as space-saving as they seem). Grow them in tower pots, strawberry pots or strawberry barrels to pack in as many plants as possible for a given area of floor space. This also makes a more decorative feature of them.

Many other fruits *can* be grown in a small garden, and even in containers, but unless you are a fruit freak, confine them to a kitchen-garden area or give them a miss. You can't have a fruit farm in a small garden, and most of us will want to concentrate on plants that look beautiful or have year-round appeal.

This pot-grown peach tree is used as an ornamental in spring. This particular flush of blossom was followed by over 40 fruits setting! Intentional and natural thinning reduced this to half a dozen superb peaches.

These redcurrants and gooseberries are part of a small collection of fruit grown in plastic tubs. They provide enough fruit to enjoy straight from the bush as a treat.

Herbs

How you integrate herbs into your garden will probably depend on whether for you herbs are a hobby in their own right or just a useful flavouring to use from time to time.

If you find herbs fascinating, and are interested in their medicinal and cosmetic uses, for example, and use them extensively in the kitchen, a herb garden would probably appeal. A herb garden can make a very attractive feature for a small garden, and could even be its centrepiece.

There are many styles of herb garden, most of them formal in outline. Herb-garden designs are a subject in their own right, and it's worth consulting specialist books on the subject. As one example, if space is very limited and most of the garden is paved, you could try the 'chequerboard' method, where every alternate paving slab is left out and the space planted with a different herb.

Most of us are content to integrate a few herbs into the general planting scheme, and fortunately many herbs are desirable as ornamentals. The majestic **angelica**, for example, is frequently grown for its 'architectural' merit by gardeners with no intention of using it as a confection. **Fennel** is another herb widely grown in borders for the beauty of its feathery foliage.

Common or **wild marjoram** (*Origanum vulgare*) is well worth a place in a border as an ornamental, and the bees and butterflies will appreciate it too. The **golden marjoram** (*O. v.* 'Aureum') makes a particularly beautiful edging plant, though **chives** can look even more stunning as a flowering edging to a flower bed or border.

Thymes have a use as ground cover, as feature plants in the rock garden, and even at the edge of a mixed border.

Containers

There's plenty of scope with containers. **Bay** is sometimes grown as a shaped and clipped tub plant, **parsley** can be grown as a ball of foliage in a hanging basket, and **mint** is great with its roots confined in a growing bag (it limits their opportunity to go exploring).

Troughs, tubs, and window-boxes can all be planted with a collection of herbs, but bear in mind that they may not look so impressive once you start to harvest them!

It's surprising what a large collection of herbs you can grow in containers — these are just a few of the herbs that the author grows on his patio.

73

A shaped bay (Laurus nobilis) *like this is really decorative. You probably won't want to spoil its shape by harvesting too many leaves!*

Opposite: Aubrieta deltoidea
'Magnificent'

Selective shortlist

There are thousands of excellent plants suitable for small gardens. There are more than 100 varieties of roses that you could use, at least 100 admirable alpines, and just as many beautiful bulbs. A whole book of this size could be filled with appropriate bedding plants for a small garden. So the plants suggested here are only a very small 'taster' of what you can grow.

Small and selective lists can be particularly useful, however, if you are a beginner. Being confronted by hundreds of roses or rhododendrons to choose from is bewildering, and there's as much chance of choosing an inferior variety as a first-rate one. A shortlist of some of the best can be invaluable and it means you start off with some really reliable basic plants. As experience grows you can add more to reflect your own preferences and gardening taste.

The plants listed here are all readily available from garden centres, though of course you may have to shop around a little as no garden centre stocks everything. You will also experience seasonal variations in availability.

Heights are given as a very approximate guide only. They are based on what you might expect after ten years for a tree or shrub, or within a season or two for other plants. Bear in mind that soil and climate affect height and growth rate, and after ten years of growth a tree in one garden could be twice the size of what it would have been in another.

Within each section, the plants are listed in alphabetical order of their botanical names. Where only the genus is shown, this includes its species, varieties and hybrids.

Small broadleaved trees

Young's weeping birch
Betula pendula 'Youngii'

Features: Graceful weeping branches. Quick-growing, but not as tall as most birches.

Likely height: 10 ft (3 m).

Special requirements: None. Will grow in most soils.

Cornus kousa

Features: A slow-growing multi-merit tree. Star-like white flowers (actually they are bracts and not petals) in late May and June. Usually bronze and crimson foliage in autumn. On mature plants strawberry-like red fruits are a bonus.

Likely height: 8 ft (2.4 m).

Special requirements: Needs a moist but well-drained soil to do well. Don't plant on shallow chalky soil.

Midland hawthorn
Crataegus oxyacantha (now more correctly *C. laevigata*)

Features: The Midland hawthorn is useful because it remains small and compact. Flowers are the main feature, double and red in the popular 'Paul's Scarlet', double and pink in 'Rosea Flore Pleno'. Some have attractive red berries in autumn.

Likely height: 10 ft (3 m).

Special requirements: Undemanding, and useful for difficult sites.

Weeping purple beech
Fagus sylvatica 'Purpurea Pendula'

Features: Weeping habit, small size (despite being a beech) and dark purple foliage.

Likely height: 7 ft (2.1 m).

Special requirements: Avoid heavy clay soil, and grow in full sun to make the most of the foliage colour. Shows off better as an isolated specimen in a lawn than at the back of a border.

Golden chain tree
Laburnum × watereri 'Vossii'

Features: Long drooping tassels of bright yellow flowers in early June. This hybrid produces few seeds, which makes it a good choice if you are worried about the possibility of children being tempted by the poisonous seeds. Quick-growing.

Likely height: 12 ft (3.7 m).

Special requirements: Undemanding and will even grow well on dry, chalky soil.

Fagus sylvatica 'Purpurea Pendula', the weeping purple beech

Flowering crab apple
Malus floribunda

Features: The tree is covered with pale pink to white flowers towards the end of April. Small yellow fruits are sometimes produced. There are also *Malus* hybrids suitable for a small garden: some are grown for their fruit, e.g. 'John Downie', others for their brighter flowers and coppery-crimson foliage, e.g. 'Profusion'.

Likely height: 10 ft (3 m).

Special requirements: Undemanding, but they do best in full sun. Avoid poorly drained soil.

Flagpole cherry
Prunus 'Amanogawa'

Features: Narrow, columnar growth, providing height without taking up much ground space. This also means less shade is cast. Single or semi-double pale pink flowers in mid- or late spring. Often good autumn colour.

Likely height: 12 ft (3.7 m).

Special requirements: Sunny position. Needs a well-drained, fertile soil; tolerates chalky soil.

Weeping willow-leafed pear
Pyrus salicifolia 'Pendula'

Features: Forms a weeping mound of silvery-grey foliage, usually with branches reaching the ground. Inconspicuous white flowers in mid-spring.

Likely height: 10 ft (3 m).

Special requirements: Very undemanding, and useful for difficult positions, but best in full sun.

Kilmarnock willow
Salix caprea 'Pendula' (now more correctly *S.* 'Kilmarnock')

Features: Weeping branches that reach the ground. Decorative catkins in early spring.

Likely height: 8 ft (2.4 m).

Flowering crab apple, Malus floribunda

Special requirements: Will grow in most soils, but does best in moist, fertile soil. Prefers full sun.

Camperdown elm
Ulmus glabra 'Camperdownii'

Features: Mushroom-shaped weeping tree with densely packed branches that reach the ground. Attractive outline even in winter when the leaves have fallen.

Likely height: 8 ft (2.4 m).

Special requirements: Undemanding; will do as well in light shade as in sun.

Prunus 'Amanogawa'

Small conifers

Chamaecyparis lawsoniana 'Ellwood's Gold'

Features: Makes a slow-growing, stubby column. Not a true gold, but the tips of the shoots are tinged yellow, particularly in summer.

Likely height: 6 ft (1.8 m).

Special requirements: Undemanding, but avoid very dry soil or shade.

Chamaecyparis obtusa 'Nana Gracilis'

Features: Distinctive, almost shell-shaped, sprays of foliage. Dark green but not dull. Unlikely to outgrow its space.

Likely height: 2 ft (60 cm).

Special requirements: Undemanding, but avoid very dry soil or shade.

Chamaecyparis pisifera 'Filifera Aurea Nana'

Features: Makes a mound of golden thread-like foliage.

Likely height: 2½ ft (75 cm).

Special requirements: Undemanding, but avoid very dry soil or shade.

Juniperus communis 'Depressa Aurea'

Features: Bright golden colour and ground-hugging habit. Will spread to 8 ft (2.4 m) or more in time.

Likely height: 3 ft (90 cm).

Special requirements: Undemanding. Will tolerate chalky soil and is relatively drought-tolerant.

Juniperus scopulorum 'Skyrocket'

Features: Very narrow column of growth, ideal where you need moderate height without sacrificing much ground space. Blue-grey foliage.

Likely height: 8 ft (2.4 m).

Special requirements: Undemanding. Will tolerate chalky and dry soil.

Right: Juniperus scopulorum *'Skyrocket'*
Below: Chamaecyparis pisifera *'Filifera Aurea Nana'*

Juniperus squamata 'Blue Star'

Features: Silver–blue foliage in summer, deeper blue–green in winter. Prostrate but will not spread too rampantly.

Likely height: 1½ ft (45 cm).

Special requirements: Undemanding. Will tolerate chalky and dry soil.

Juniperus squamata *'Blue Star'*

Special requirements: Undemanding provided drainage is good.

Thuja orientalis 'Aurea Nana'

Features: Oval-shaped with yellowish-gold summer foliage, bronzy in winter.

Likely height: 2 ft (60 cm).

Special requirements: Undemanding provided drainage is good.

Picea glauca albertina 'Conica'

Features: Distinctive cone shape. Slow-growing. Bright green foliage.

Likely height: 3 ft (90 cm).

Special requirements: Avoid dry, chalky or shallow soil.

Irish yew
Taxus baccata 'Fastigiata Aurea'

Features: Narrow column of golden foliage. Slow-growing but very striking.

Likely height: 6 ft (1.8 m).

Special requirements: Undemanding, but drainage must be good. Tolerates shade but colour is best in sun.

Thuja occidentalis 'Rheingold'

Features: Rounded to conical shape. Old-gold colour in summer, turning coppery in winter.

Likely height: 4 ft (1.2 m).

Thuja orientalis *'Aurea Nana'*

Evergreen shrubs

Mexican orange blossom
Choisya ternata 'Sundance'

Features: Bright yellow foliage; white, fragrant flowers in late spring.

Likely height: 6 ft (1.8 m)

Special requirements: Best in a sheltered position. Leaves may be damaged by winter cold, but if cut out, new growth usually restores the former beauty.

Rock rose
Cistus × purpureus

Features: Eye-catching rosy-crimson single flowers in early and mid-summer. Other species and varieties are pink or white.

Likely height: 4 ft (1.2 m). Some other species and hybrids are smaller.

Special requirements: Full sun and well-drained soil. Not totally hardy, so take cuttings in summer as insurance.

Elaeagnus pungens 'Maculata'

Features: Bright yellow centres to the leathery leaves. Its golden variegation will light up a winter garden.

Likely height: 8 ft (2.4 m).

Special requirements: Un-demanding, but choose a position where it will catch the winter sun.

Winter heather
Erica carnea

Features: Heathers need no description, and there are many kinds beside this one. The many *E. carnea* varieties flower from mid-winter to mid-spring.

Likely height: 1½ ft (45 cm).

Special requirements: Most heathers require an acid soil, but this one will tolerate neutral or even slightly alkaline soil. Will tolerate partial shade, but best in full sun.

Euonymus fortunei

Features: There are several good varieties with attractively variegated foliage. Low-growing and makes good ground cover, but can also be trained up a wall.

Likely height: 1½ ft (45 cm) as ground cover.

Special requirements: Un-demanding. Will tolerate sun or shade, but variegation and colouring is usually better in sun.

Hebe

Features: Mounds of neat foliage, though some are ground-hugging. Many have attractive (usually blue or purple) flowers late in the season. *H. pinguifolia* 'Pagei' is a silver-grey foliaged ground-hugger with white flowers.

Likely height: Varies with species and variety.

Choisya ternata *'Sundance'*

Erica carnea *'Myretoun Ruby'*

Special requirements: Undemanding regarding soil but best in good light. Unfortunately many are not dependably hardy in cold areas, which is why specific ones have not been suggested. Check with your garden centre for which ones arc likely to be reliable in your area. They are well worth the trouble.

Sun rose, rock rose
Helianthemum nummularium

Features: Masses of flowers between late spring and midsummer. There are many varieties and hybrids in shades of pink, red, orange, yellow and white.

Likely height: 1 ft (30 cm).

Special requirements: Good drainage and full sun. Tolerates chalky soil.

Mahonia **'Charity'**

Features: Large, glossy leaves attractive the year round, topped by sprays of fragrant yellow flowers in winter.

Likely height: 10 ft (3 m); growth habit is tall and narrow.

Special requirements: Undemanding.

Rhododendron **(including azaleas)**

Features: Rhododendrons and azaleas are grown for their masses of flowers, usually in late spring. But there are many hundreds of kinds ranging from dwarfs of 1 ft (30 cm) to huge shrubs totally unsuitable for a small garden. Ask for advice regarding suitability for a small garden when you purchase. Most described as Yakushimanum hybrids, of which there are many varieties, should be suitable.

Likely height: Depends on variety.

Special requirements: Needs an acid soil. Do not attempt to grow on chalky soil. If your soil is unsuitable, try growing in a large container filled with an ericaceous (acid) compost.

Yucca flaccida **'Ivory'**

Features: Rosette of stiff, sword-like leaves. Tall flower spike with large white bells, in mid- or late summer.

Likely height: 5 ft (1.5 m) in flower.

Special requirements: Avoid heavy clay soil. Tolerates semi-shade but is best in full sun.

Yucca flaccida *'Ivory'*

Deciduous shrubs

Barberry
Berberis thunbergii
'Atropurpurea Nana'

Features: Mound of dark bronze-purple leaves. Good autumn colour.

Likely height: 2 ft (60 cm). Also worth growing are 'Aurea' (5 ft/1.5 m), 'Bagatelle' (1½ ft/ 45 cm), and 'Helmond Pillar' (4 ft/1.2m, but narrow).

Special requirements: Un-demanding and will grow in most conditions.

Blue spiraea
Caryopteris × clandonensis

Features: Bright blue flowers in late summer and early autumn. Grey-green foliage.

Likely height: 3 ft (90 cm).

Special requirements: May be cut back in a hard winter, but usually regrows freely from base. Tolerates chalky soil.

Hardy plumbago
Ceratostigma willmottianum

Features: Masses of pale blue flowers in summer and early autumn. Good foliage colour before the leaves drop.

Likely height: 3 ft (90 cm).

Special requirements: Best in a sheltered position. Top may be killed in a cold winter, but it will usually regrow from the base. Likes dry, chalky soil.

Dogwood
Cornus alba

Features: Popularly grown for red winter stems (greenish-yellow in the similar *C. stolonifera* 'Flaviramea'). Some, such as 'Elegantissima' and 'Spaethii', have variegated foliage.

Caryopteris × clandonensis

Berberis thunbergii *'Atropurpurea Nana'*

Likely height: 5 ft (1.5 m).

Special requirements: Un-demanding. Will do well in partial shade or full sun.

Broom
Cytisus × praecox

Features: Masses of pale-yellow pea-type flowers (darker in 'Allgold') in spring.

Likely height: 2½ ft (75 cm).

Special requirements: Good drainage — does well in sandy soil. Full sun.

Mezereon
Daphne mezereum

Features: Very fragrant pur-plish-red flowers in late winter and early spring on bare stems. Poisonous berries may follow.

Likely height: 4 ft (1.2 m).

Special requirements: Needs a humus-rich soil. Will thrive in partial shade or full sun.

Golden bell bush
Forsythia × intermedia 'Lynwood'

Features: This very popular yellow-flowered shrub is a familiar sight in early or mid-spring. This variety has large flowers with broad petals.

Likely height: 8 ft (2.4 m).

Special requirements: Undemanding, but best in full sun.

Hardy fuchsia
Fuchsia magellanica

Features: Long, thin-petalled flowers of typical fuchsia shape and colour. There are also variegated varieties.

Likely height: 5 ft (1.5 m), taller in frost-free areas.

Special requirements: Tolerates a wide range of soils, but

Potentilla fruticosa *'Abbotswood'*

is best in one that is moisture-retentive and fertile. Top growth may be killed by frost, but the plant usually regrows from the base in spring.

Tree hollyhock
Hibiscus syriacus

Features: Large flowers shaped like those of a hollyhock, in shades of blue, pink or white, in late summer and early autumn. There are single, semi-double and double varieties.

Likely height: 8 ft (2.4 m).

Special requirements: Requires good drainage and a sunny position.

Shrubby potentilla
Potentilla fruticosa

Features: Small single flowers in shades of yellow, orange, red and white, from early summer to early autumn. There are many varieties.

Likely height: 4 ft (1.2 m) (most varieties).

Special requirements: Undemanding, but try to avoid poorly draining soil. Will tolerate partial shade, but best in full sun.

Fuchsia magellanica *'Variegata'*

Climbers and wall shrubs

Japonica or ornamental quince
Chaenomeles speciosa

Features: Red, pink, orange or white flowers in late winter though spring. Sometimes grown as a free-standing bush, but best trained against a wall or fence.

Likely height: 6 ft (1.8 m).

Special requirements: Undemanding and will grow well in partial shade or full sun.

Clematis (large-flowered hybrids)

Features: Grown for their large flowers, usually brightly coloured. Flowering is mainly early summer to early autumn, according to variety. Avoid the small-flowered, rampant species such as *C. montana* unless you are prepared to restrict the growth or have the space to let them have their head.

Likely height: 10 ft (3 m).

Special requirements: To do well they need moist, fertile ground. Although they will flower very well in full sun, their roots should be shaded if possible. They grow well on chalky soil.

Herringbone cotoneaster
Cotoneaster horizontalis

Features: Bright red berries in autumn, lasting into early winter. Good autumn colour before the leaves drop. White flowers in late spring or early summer are a bonus.

Likely height: 6 ft (1.8 m) against a wall (will also make a ground-cover shrub).

Special requirements: Undemanding and will grow well in most soils, in sun or partial shade.

Silk tassel bush
Garrya elliptica 'James Roof'

Features: A winter-interest evergreen with long catkins (sometimes over 1 ft/30 cm long) in mid- and late winter.

Likely height: 8 ft (2.4 m).

Special requirements: Tolerant of a wide range of soils and will do well on chalk. Vulnerable in very cold gardens, so is often grown against a wall for protection.

Ivy
Hedera helix

Features: Evergreen foliage plant known by almost everyone. There are many different varieties, with a range of leaf shapes, some variegated.

Likely height: Roof height if not restricted. Can also be used as ground cover.

Clematis 'Lasurstern' and 'Nelly Moser'

Cotoneaster horizontalis

Special requirements: Undemanding, and will grow in any normal garden soil, in full sun to full shade. Variegated varieties are best in full sun or partial shade.

Winter jasmine
Jasminum nudiflorum

Features: Small but very bright yellow flowers produced over a very long period — starting in late autumn and continuing until late winter.

Likely height: 10 ft (3 m).

Special requirements: Undemanding and will grow in any normal garden soil, in sun or shade. If possible, avoid a position where early morning sun will thaw the frozen flowers too rapidly.

Opposite: Garrya elliptica

Common jasmine
Jasminum officinale 'Aureum'

Features: White to pink fragrant flowers in late summer. Green and gold variegated semi-evergreen leaves.

Likely height: 10 ft (3 m).

Special requirements: Undemanding regarding soil, but not very hardy. Grow in a warm, sunny position.

Honeysuckle
Lonicera × brownii 'Dropmore Scarlet'

Features: Clusters of orange-red flowers in early and mid-summer. Although a kind of honeysuckle, this one is not fragrant.

Likely height: 8 ft (2.4 m).

Special requirements: Undemanding regarding soil, and will grow in sun or partial shade.

Firethorn
Pyracantha

Features: Red or orange berries in autumn, lasting into winter. White flowers in early summer are a bonus. Can be grown as a free-standing shrub but usually seen trained against a wall.

Likely height: 10 ft (3 m).

Special requirements: Undemanding, and tolerates chalky soil. Will perform well in sun or partial shade.

Rose (climbing)
Rosa

Features: There are many varieties, all grown for their beautiful and usually fragrant blooms. They flower in early summer, and sometimes throughout summer (according to variety). Select varieties that appeal to you personally.

Likely height: About 10 ft (3 m).

Special requirements: Undemanding regarding soil, and will tolerate some shade, but best in a position that receives plenty of sun.

Jasminum nudiflorum

Herbaceous plants

The plants in this list are more appropriately described as border plants, or plants for a herbaceous (or mixed) border, for some are non-woody evergreens. They do not die back to the ground in winter to leave bare soil, like a typical herbaceous plant. Non-woody evergreens are particularly useful as they help to give the borders a clothed appearance even in winter.

Bugle
Ajuga reptans

Features: Grown for foliage effect, many varieties having variegated and attractively coloured foliage. Practically evergreen. Carpeting habit, useful as ground cover at the front of a border.

Likely height: 4 in (10 cm).

Special requirements: Undemanding. Will grow in sun or partial shade.

Lady's mantle
Alchemilla mollis

Features: Sprays of tiny yellowish-green flowers in summer. The pale-green hairy leaves are also attractive, especially when they catch and hold drops of rain or dew.

Likely height: 1½ ft (45 cm).

Special requirements: Undemanding. Will grow in sun or partial shade.

Michaelmas daisy
Aster novi-belgii

Features: Useful for late flowering, usually in September and October when little else is in bloom in the border.

Likely height: 2–4 ft (60–120 cm), according to variety.

Special requirements: Best in full sun. Do not overcrowd the plants. Keep an eye open for early signs of mildew, then treat promptly.

Elephant ears
Bergenia cordifolia

Features: Deep-pink flowers in spring; also worth growing for foliage effect. Large, thick, evergreen leaves, often turning reddish in winter. There are other similar species and varieties in various shades of pink, red and white.

Likely height: 1½ ft (45 cm).

Special requirements: Undemanding. Does well in sun or shade, but prefers good drainage.

Sedge
Carex morrowii 'Evergold'

Features: Bright evergreen variegated green and gold grass-like leaves.

Likely height: 1 ft (30 cm).

Special requirements: Avoid dry soil.

Aster novi-belgii *'Jenny'*

Ajuga reptans *'Atropurpurea'*

Elephant ears (Bergenia cordifolia)

Pink
Dianthus allwoodii

Features: Fragrant pink, red or white flowers in early summer. Grey evergreen foliage.

Likely height: 1 ft (30 cm).

Special requirements: Will grow in most soils, but does particularly well on chalky soil. Best in full sun.

Christmas and Lenten roses
Helleborus

Features: Grown for their early flowers, usually white and in December or January with the Christmas rose (*H. niger*), mainly various shades of pinks and purples and in February or March with the Lenten rose (*H. orientalis*).

Likely height: 1 ft (30 cm).

Special requirements: Needs moist but well-drained soil that will not dry out. Prefers shade.

Plantain lily
Hosta

Features: Although flowers are a bonus in mid- and late summer, hostas are grown primarily as foliage plants. There are scores of good varieties, many with variegated or golden leaves. Choose one that appeals, but avoid the very large varieties.

Likely height: Most varieties 1–2 ft (30–60 cm).

Special requirements: Very undemanding and will grow in full sun or full shade. Slugs are a problem so be prepared to control them, especially in spring as the leaves unfurl.

Beard tongue
Penstemon

Features: Flower spikes with nodding bell flowers, not unlike a miniature foxglove. There are varieties in many colours, mainly reds, pinks and purples, but also white. They have the merit of a particularly long flowering season from early summer into autumn.

Likely height: 2–2½ ft (60–75 cm), according to variety.

Special requirements: Best in a soil that drains freely without

drying out, and in full sun. They are of borderline hardiness in very cold areas, in which case it is worth overwintering in a cold frame or taking cuttings to overwinter in a more protected environment.

Polygonatum affine

Features: Useful carpeter with pink poker-like flower heads that last for a long time, often from early summer into early autumn. There are several good varieties, with flowers in various shade of pink to almost red.

Likely height: 1 ft (30 cm).

Special requirements: Undemanding. Will thrive in full sun or partial shade.

London pride
Saxifraga × urbium

Features: Sprays of small starry pink flowers carried well above ground-hugging rosettes of evergreen foliage. *S. umbrosa primuloides* is similar and particularly good.

Likely height: 1 ft (30 cm).

Special requirements: Does best in a fertile soil in partial shade. Avoid a position in full sun for long periods.

Penstemon *'Chester Scarlet'*

Rock-garden plants

Gold dust
Alyssum saxatile (now more correctly *Aurinia saxatilis*)

Features: Bright yellow flowers in mid- and late spring.

Likely height: 9 in (23 cm).

Special requirements: Good drainage and full sun. Can be rampant, so trim back immediately after flowering.

Common thrift
Armeria maritima

Features: Small 'drumstick' heads of pink, red or white flowers in late spring and early summer. Grass-like evergreen foliage.

Likely height: 9 in (23 cm).

Special requirements: Good drainage and full sun.

Alyssum saxatile

Rock cress
Aubrieta deltoidea

Features: A carpet of flowers in shades of blue, purple, red or pink, in mid- and late spring. There are many varieties and hybrids from which to choose.

Likely height: 6 in (15 cm).

Special requirements: Good drainage and full sun. Can be rampant, so trim back immediately after flowering.

Garland flower
Daphne cneorum

Features: Fragrant pink flowers in mid- and late spring. There is also a variety of this dwarf shrub with the bonus of variegated leaves.

Likely height: 9 in (23 cm).

Special requirements: Fertile soil with plenty of humus (from garden compost or rotted manure, for example). Best in full sun.

Perennial candytuft
Iberis sempervirens

Features: Clusters of white flowers in late spring or early summer over evergreen foliage.

Likely height: 9 in (23 cm); 4 in (10 cm) for 'Little Gem'.

Special requirements: Well-drained soil and full sun.

Oxalis adenophylla

Features: Pretty pink flowers over attractive grey-green leaves.

Likely height: 4 in (10 cm).

Special requirements: Well-drained soil in full sun.

Rock phlox
Phlox subulata

Features: Carpet of bright red, pink or blue flowers in late spring and early summer. There are several good varieties in a range of colours.

Likely height: 6 in (15 cm).

Armeria maritima

Special requirements: Does best in well-drained soil that does not dry out completely, and in full sun.

Saxifrage
Saxifraga

Features: There are many different kinds of saxifrage for the rock garden; most are grown for their pretty flowers over moss-like hummocks of foliage in spring, others for their foliage effect. Be guided by personal preferences.

Likely height: 4 in (10 cm), though some may be taller.

Special requirements: Well-drained soil is essential. Some sun is appreciated, but many prefer a little shade when the sun is at its hottest.

Stonecrop
Sedum spathulifolium 'Cape Blanco'

Features: Like most of this large group of rock plants, this

Saxifraga *'Peter Pan'*

variety has attractive foliage (silver-grey) and flowers (bright yellow). Be prepared to explore other rock sedums too.

Likely height: 3 in (7.5 cm).

Special requirements: Good drainage and full sun.

Houseleek
Sempervivum

Features: There are many species and hybrids, all with interesting foliage rosettes. Some have unusual flowers on long stems. It is possible to have a whole collection of these in a small area.

Likely height: About 3 in (7.5 cm) without flowers, up to about 1 ft (30 cm) with flowers, though it depends on the species or variety.

Special requirements: Good drainage.

Phlox subulata *'Alexander's Surprise'*

Patio and dwarf roses

'Petit Four'

In all but the smallest gardens you will have space to grow a few of the normal 'full-sized' hybrid tea and floribunda roses. The varieties described here have floribunda-type flowers, but are more compact than normal varieties and are suitable for smaller beds or for growing on the patio (in containers or in small beds and borders). You can, of course, use true miniature roses, but these are generally less showy.

Unless otherwise stated, the varieties below grow to about 1-2 ft (30-60 cm) with normal pruning. Some may also be available as standards.

'Conservation'

Coral pink flowers and glossy foliage. Good fragrance. Bushy growth.

'Flower Carpet'

Bright pink flowers on prostrate stems. Can be used as ground cover, in baskets, or in ordinary tubs and large pots.

Below: *'Peek A Boo'*

Below: *'Sweet Dream'* as a patio standard

'Robin Redbreast'

'Robin Redbreast'

Red flowers with a white eye. It looks striking as an edging to a border. Can also be used for ground cover.

'Sweet Dream'

Cup-shaped deep apricot to peach flowers. Try it in small beds or borders, or in tubs. It will make a wonderful patio standard!

'Sweet Magic'

Glowing orange with gold tints. Fragrant flowers on a compact plant.

'Top Marks'

Bright, vibrant vermilion double blooms, flowering over a long period. Effective massed in a bed instead of summer bedding plants.

'Nozomi'

Clusters of profuse pale pink to almost white single flowers. A useful ground-cover rose for a small garden, and can be effective in containers. It will cascade if planted in a tub, and is sometimes budded to make a small standard.

'Peek A Boo'

Masses of apricot to pink flowers with pointed buds. Rounded and slightly spreading growth.

'Petit Four'

Small, single pink flowers on a compact plant.

'Sweet Magic'   **Right:** *'Top Marks'*

'Warm Welcome'

Here's a patio climber to go with your other patio roses. It will grow to about 8 ft (2.4 m), perhaps up a pillar or against a wall. The flowers are a striking orange.

Bulbs and corms

Anemone blanda

Features: Masses of usually blue (sometimes pink or white) daisy-like flowers in spring. Naturalises easily.

Likely height: 4 in (10 cm).

Special requirements: Does best in fertile and well-drained soil that does not dry out completely. Suitable for full sun or partial shade. Will even grow beneath trees.

Anemone blanda *'Blue Shades'*

Glory of the snow
Chionodoxa luciliae

Features: Small sprays of star-like flowers, pale blue with white centres. Multiplies and naturalises freely. There is also a pink variety. Sometimes flowers in late winter but usually early spring.

Likely height: 6 in (15 cm).

Special requirements: Tolerant of most soil, and will grow in sun or partial shade.

Autumn crocus
Colchicum autumnale

Features: Grown for the large crocus-like flowers in autumn (before the leaves). The leaves appear in spring.

Likely height: 9 in (23 cm) in flower (leaves taller).

Special requirements: Requires fertile, well-drained but humus-rich soil. Happy in sun or partial shade.

Crocus chrysanthus

Features: Grown for the typical crocus flowers, though these are smaller than the large-flowered type. They can be naturalised in grass or allowed to grow into large clumps in a border.

Likely height: 3 in (7.5 cm).

Special requirements: Undemanding. Well-drained soil, in sun or partial shade.

Common snowdrop
Galanthus nivalis

Features: The white flowers of the snowdrop in late winter or early spring require no introduction.

Likely height: 6 in (15 cm).

Special requirements: Humus-rich soil that does not dry out. Best in partial shade.

Hyacinth
Hyacinthus

Features: The stiff spikes of the hyacinth are known to almost all gardeners. Although

Galanthus nivalis

Colchicum autumnale

often grown in pots and bowls, they make good garden plants to flower in spring. They can even be left to naturalise and multiply.

Likely height: 9 in (23 cm).

Special requirements: Humus-rich soil that does not dry out. Best in sun or partial shade.

Spring starflower
Ipheion uniflorum

Features: Masses of pale blue flowers (deeper in 'Wisley Blue') in mid- and late spring. Will soon multiply if left undisturbed.

Likely height: 6 in (15 cm).

Special requirements: Undemanding. Best in well-drained soil in sun or partial shade.

Grape hyacinth
Muscari armeniacum

Features: Blue flower spikes, resembling a small hyacinth. Multiplies freely and makes attractive drifts or a pretty edging to a bed or border.

Likely height: 9 in (23 cm).

Special requirements: Undemanding, but best in well-drained soil and sun.

Daffodil
Narcissus

Features: Everyone knows the common yellow trumpet daffodil, but there are varieties with short cups instead of long trumpets, in white and pink as well as yellow. There are also doubles and 'orchid-flowered'

types with no separate cup or trumpet. If space is really limited there are dozens of miniatures. All will multiply and make larger clumps if left undisturbed.

Likely height: 4-24 in (10-60 cm), according to variety.

Special requirements: Undemanding. Will grow in sun or shade.

Muscari armeniacum

Nerine bowdenii

Features: Clusters of spidery pink flowers on long, leafless stems, from early to late autumn and sometimes into early winter.

Likely height: 2 ft (60 cm).

Special requirements: Well-drained soil and a warm, sunny position are essential. Easy to grow in mild areas, more difficult in cold regions. Leave undisturbed to form large clumps.

93

Container plants

Fibrous-rooted begonia
Begonia semperflorens

Features: Mounds of red, pink or white flowers over glossy green, bronze or reddish leaves. Will flower from early summer until the first frost.

Likely height: 6–12 in (15–30 cm), according to variety.

Special requirements: Undemanding. Best in partial shade, but will tolerate sun or shade.

Marguerite
Argyranthemum

Features: Daisy-like flowers over feathery foliage from mid-summer. There are many varieties in shades of pink and yellow as well as white. More suitable for tubs than for windowboxes.

Likely height: 2 ft (60 cm).

Fuchsia in pot

Begonia semperflorens

Special requirements: Undemanding, but best in full sun. Although perennial, the plants are too tender to be left out. Overwinter the plants, or cuttings from them, under glass.

Fuchsia

Features: Fuchsias need no description, their pendant flowers being very popular. There are, however, many kinds, including singles and doubles, bush forms, standards, and cascaders. The last are ideal for hanging baskets or the front of other containers.

Likely height: 1–3 ft (30–90cm).

Special requirements: Any good potting soil is suitable, but they will require regular feeding as well as dead-heading to maintain flowering over most of the summer. Never

allow them to dry out. The types used in containers are not hardy and must be over-wintered under glass (the old plant or cuttings from it).

Busy lizzie
Impatiens hybrids and varieties

Features: Most are grown for their non-stop prolific flowers, mainly in shades of red, orange and pink, as well as white. Flowering starts in early summer and continues until the first frost kills the plants. There are many varieties, which vary considerably in size and growth habit, so choose one appropriate to the container. Some of the New Guinea hybrids have variegated foliage.

Likely height: 6–12 in (15–30 cm), most varieties.

Special requirements: Undemanding. Will grow in full sun or in shade.

Lobelia

Features: The trailing varieties are popular for hanging baskets or the front of windowboxes, but the bushy types are also worth growing in containers of all kinds. They will flower for months unless you let them dry out. Although blue is the main colour, there are also red- and white-flowered varieties, and mixtures.

Likely height: 6 in (15 cm) or less.

Special requirements: Undemanding, provided the potting soil is kept moist. Will grow well in full sun or partial shade.

Geranium
Pelargonium

Features: Traditional and very popular flowers for containers of all kinds. There are many types, including trailers and bush types, and even miniatures. Most will flower from early summer to the first frost. Regal pelargoniums (*P. × domesticum*) are not suitable for outdoor containers.

Likely height: Trailing, or to 1½ ft (45 cm), according to variety.

Special requirements: Undemanding, but best in sun. Overwinter under glass, or buy or raise fresh plants each year.

Petunia

Features: There are many varieties of petunia, all grown for their profusion of flowers in many colours. Perhaps the most spectacular for containers, and especially hanging

Impatiens in a strawberry pot

baskets, is the Surfinia range. These have trailing growth, and are covered with flowers for practically the whole summer. In some Surfinia varieties the flowers are slightly fragrant.

Likely height: Trailing to 1½ ft (45 cm), according to variety.

Special requirements: Undemanding, but keep well fed and watered to sustain the prolific blooming.

French marigold
Tagetes patula

Features: Mass of flowers over several months, mainly yellow and orange shades. There are double, semi-double and singles. Often in flower before they are planted.

Likely height: 4–12 in (10–30 cm), according to variety.

Special requirements: Undemanding, but best in full sun.

Pansy
Viola × wittrockiana

Features: Pansies need no description, and they will be found in containers almost every month of the year. The winter-flowering varieties will bloom whenever the weather is not too severe, but most

Ivy-leafed geranium in porch

prolifically in late winter and early spring. Other varieties are at their best in summer and autumn containers.

Likely height: 6–9 in (15–23 cm).

Special requirements: Undemanding, but feed, water and deadhead them regularly to keep the flowers coming.

Verbena

Features: Masses of flowers in a range of colours. There are both seed-raised and vegetatively propagated varieties. The latter are often the best for a container display.

Likely height: 6–12 in (15–30 cm).

Special requirements: Grows best in well-drained soil and full sun.

Index

Acer 30
Ajuga 60, 86
Alchemilla 86
Alyssum 88
Anemone 92
Anthemis 34-35
apples 22, 71, 77
arbours 51
Argyranthemum 94
Armeria 38, 88
Aster 86
Aubrieta 75, 88
Aurinia 88
barberry 82
bay 73, 74
beans 68, 69
beard tongue 87
beds 41-45, 49
beech 22, 76
beetroot 69
Begonia 94
Berberis 32, 82
Bergenia 86
birch (*Betula*) 76
bird-of-paradise flower 63
blackcurrants 72
borders 41-45, 69-70
boundaries 8, 24-32
broom 82
bugle 86
bulbs 92-93
busy lizzie 67, 94
cabbages 69
Carex 60, 86
carrots 70
Caryopteris 82
cauliflowers 69
celery 69
Ceratostigma 45, 82
Chaenomeles 84
Chamaecyparis 78
chamomile 34-35, 62
cherry, flagpole 22, 77
Chionodoxa 92
Chlorophytum 67
Choisya 80
Cistus 80
Clematis 49, 84
climbers 84-85
Colchicum 92
computers, use of 13
container plants 94-95
containers 48-49, 56-60, 73
corms 92-93

Cornus 44, 76, 82
Cotoneaster 50, 84
Cotula 35
courgettes 69
Crataegus 76
Crocus 92
cucumbers 69
Cytisus 82
daffodil 93
Daphne 82-83, 88
design 8-23
Dianthus 87
dividing a garden 18-20
dogwood 82
drain covers 40
Elaeagnus 29, 80
elephant ears 86
elm 22, 77
enclosed gardens 17-18, 47
Erica 60, 80
Euonymus 50, 60, 80
Euphorbia 60
Fagus 22, 76
fences 25-26
firethorn 85
focal points 61-62
Forsythia 83
fountains 54-55
fruits 66, 71-72
Fuchsia 83, 94
Galanthus 92
garland flower 88
Garrya 84
geraniums 95
glory of the snow 92
gold dust 88
golden bell bush 83
golden chain tree 76
golden hop 30
gooseberries 72
grape hyacinth 93
gravel 36-38
Guernsey lily 45
hanging baskets 59
hawthorn 76
heather 60, 80
Hebe 80-81
Hedera 84-85
hedges 31-32
Helianthemum 38, 81
hellebore 60
Helleborus 60, 87
herbaceous plants 86-87
herbs 73
Hibiscus 83
honeysuckle 18, 85
Hosta 87
houseleek 89

Humulus 30
hyacinth 92-93
Iberis 88
Impatiens 94
inspiration 13-14
Ipheion 93
ivy 84-85
japonica 84
jasmine (*Jasminum*) 50, 85
juniper (*Juniperus*) 78
kitchen gardens 66-74
Laburnum 76
lady's mantle 86
Laurus 74
lawns 34-35
lettuces 69, 70
lighting 64-65
Ligustrum 31
Lobelia 94-95
London pride 87
Lonicera 85
Mahonia 81
Malus 22, 77
maple 30
marguerite 94
marigold, French 95
marjoram 73
measuring/marking 13, 16
Mexican orange blossom 80
mezereon 82-83
Michaelmas daisy 86
mint 73
mirrors 20-21
Muscari 93
Narcissus 93
Nerine 45, 93
Oenothera 38
open-plan gardens 17-18
optical illusions 20-21, 29
Origanum 73
ornaments 61-65
Oxalis 88
Pachysandra 35, 44
pansy 95
parsley 73
Parthenocissus 50
patios 29, 46-50
paving 39, 47-48
peaches 72
pears 66, 71, 77
peas 68-69
Pelargonium 95
Penstemon 87
Petunia 95
Phlox 88-89
Picea 79
pinks 87
planning 5-6

plantain lily 87
Polygonatum 87
ponds 53-54
potatoes 68
Potentilla 83
privacy 8, 29-30
privet 31
Prunus 22, 77
Pyracantha 50, 85
Pyrus 77
quince, ornamental 84
red-hot poker 64
redcurrants 72
Rhododendron 81
rhubarb 56, 67
rock cress 88
rock-garden plants 88-89
roses 31, 85, 90-91
  Lenten/Christmas 60, 87
  rock 80, 81
Salix 22, 77
saxifrage (*Saxifraga*) 87, 89
screen-block wall 30
sedge 86
Sedum 89
Sempervivum 89
shade 8, 17
shrubs 80-85
silk tassel bush 84
snowdrop 92
soft fruits 72
Solanum 60
stonecrop 89
strawberries 72
streams 53-54
Strelitzia 63
summerhouses 51-52
Tagetes 95
Taxus 22, 79
thrift 38, 88
Thuja 79
thyme (*Thymus*) 35, 73
timber decking 38-39
tomatoes 69, 70
trees 21-22, 76-79
trellises 26
Ulmus 22, 77
using this book 7
vegetables 66, 68-70
Verbena 95
Viola 95
Virginia creeper 50
walls 27-28, 49
water features 53-55
willow 22, 77
winter displays 59-60
yew 22, 79
Yucca 81